INTEGRATION AND COMMUNITY BUILDING
IN EASTERN EUROPE

INTEGRATION AND COMMUNITY BUILDING
IN EASTERN EUROPE

Jan F. Triska, series editor

The German Democratic Republic
Arthur M. Hanhardt, Jr.

The Polish People's Republic
James F. Morrison

The Development of Socialist Yugoslavia
M. George Zaninovich

The People's Republic of Albania
Nicholas C. Pano

THE DEVELOPMENT
OF SOCIALIST YUGOSLAVIA

THE DEVELOPMENT OF SOCIALIST YUGOSLAVIA

M. GEORGE ZANINOVICH

THE JOHNS HOPKINS PRESS

Baltimore

FOREWORD

The Development of Socialist Yugoslavia is part of a series of monographs dealing with integration and community building in the communist party states of Eastern Europe. These monographs are further part of a larger program of studies of the communist system sponsored by Stanford University.

It seems appropriate here to outline the theoretical and methodological concepts that were developed for the series as a whole. The focus has been on the communist-ruled states as part of a loosely structured community or system—its origins, development, and internal behavior. The major underlying assumption is that each communist party state has characteristics peculiar to it that predispose it toward varying degrees of cooperation, co-ordination, and integration with the others. We think that the present behavioral characteristics of the system can be traced to environmental, attitudinal, and systemic factors, and that we can learn a great deal from a comparative analysis of the process and degree of integration of each member state into the community of communist party states—whether, for example, the process involves force or consent, similar or shared institutions and codes of behavior, or whether integration is effective at elite levels and/or at lower levels as well, and so on.

The concept of political integration and community formation and maintenance is, as a focus of intellectual curiosity and investigation, as old as the study of politics. The mushrooming of supranational integrational movements since World War II has given a considerable new impetus to the old curiosity and has changed the emphasis of the investigations. Social scientists, who in the last two decades have been building a general theory of political integration, whether on a subnational, national, or supranational level, have been perhaps less concerned with the philosophical content of the concept of integration than with discovering operational indicators that would endow the concept with empirical meaning and allow the theory to be tested for validity and reliability. The principal centers of their inquiry have been two broad independent variables, *interaction* and *attitude*. Although in most cases investigated separately, interaction and attitude are assumed to combine to constitute a community, the objective of the process of integration.

The principal subjects of inquiry have been transactions across the boundaries of states and attitude formation within them. The theorists stipulate that the number and density of transactions among states indicate the degree and nature of their relationships. Flow of mail and telephone traffic; trade; aid; exchange of tourists, officials, and migrants; cultural exchange of persons and communications; newspapers, periodicals, and book sales and translations; radio, TV, and motion picture exchange; mutual treaties and agreements; and common organizations and conferences are the kinds of indicators that, measured and plotted over time, should demonstrate the direction of integrational trends and developments.

With reference to attitude formation, theorists have been more concerned with the process of integration than with its results (conditions) within states. The pertinent literature yields relatively little on this subject. In *Nationalism and Social Communication,* Karl Deutsch argues that it may be fruitful to study two sets of persons within a unit of analysis: those "mobilized" for integrational communications and those "assimilated" into the new, larger unit. If those assimilated multiply at a more rapid rate than those mobilized, then "assimilation" is gaining and "community is growing faster than society."

At present enormous problems are involved in studying the results of the integration process in communist countries. It is difficult to assess attitudes because of the great sensitivity of officials and decision makers, and it is either difficult or impossible to obtain reliable aggregate and survey data. This informational problem makes it correspondingly difficult to develop a general theory of integration or to make systematic comparative analyses. We have therefore been compelled to rely on indicators of degrees and trends, a method that depends considerably on subjective judgment and inference.

Although the data available are uneven in quality and quantity, our approach has been rigorous and systematic. Each author was asked to examine the country under review with reference to five historical periods: (1) the precommunist stage before the country became a party state and hence a member of the system; (2) the period of the communists' consolidation of power after World War II when the states of Eastern Europe entered the system; (3) the subsequent era of repression and rigid controls; (4) the period of relaxed controls following Stalin's death; (5) the last ten years. For each of these periods, as appropriate, the author was asked to identify and analyze the phenomena relevant to his country's integration in the system: its ecological-physical features, its demographic structure, belief system, social system, degree of autonomy, its dependence on other states, and its hopes, needs, and expectations with regard to integration and development. Within these broad confines, each author was asked to emphasize the periods and events with the greatest significance for the integrational development of the country in question. It is our feeling that a more rigid set of prescriptions would have been self-defeating in view of our objectives and the exploratory nature of our undertaking.

Since the overriding task of Professor Zaninovich's study is to examine the role of Yugoslavia as a communist society, it can serve as a useful introduction to any student of the country. Still, as in the other studies in this series, a major focus is on that behavior of Yugoslavia relevant to integration and community formation with its neighbors and friends in Eastern Europe, in particular with the Soviet Union.

In this connection, in particular, Professor Zaninovich warns about and deplores the widespread belief that communist regimes do not essentially change, that there is some peculiar quality about them which constrains them to remain essentially the same, by themselves as well as in relations with others. Such a belief, he maintains, is both false and unfortunate. Instead, he shows that changes in communist thought and organization are not only frequent—they are often fundamental. Like all other social systems, communist party states contain the seeds of their own transformation: "Existing communist regimes (and, among them, the Yugoslav) respond to practical demands emanating from their environments in much the same way as do other states," he points out. And he sees it as his task "to observe adaptations [to . . . practical concerns] and, specifically, to detect and measure their impact within the context of the Yugoslav experience."

One final remark of a general nature is in order. The series is based on the assumption that although the countries of Eastern Europe are now gaining more freedom to conduct their own affairs, they do not reject the need for association among themselves as such. All the communist parties in power in Eastern Europe find real and necessary the idea of a world communist community united in opposing capitalism and in carrying out its historical destiny. All of them, we believe, would find it instinctively repugnant to do anything that could precipitate a final, total break with the communist system.

This series is an intellectual product of many creative minds. In addition to the authors of the individual monographs—in this case, Professor M. George Zaninovich, Department of Political Science, University of Oregon—I would like especially to thank Professor David D. Finley of The Colorado College and Stanford University for his original contribution and assistance.

Jan F. Triska

Institute of Political Studies
Stanford University

CONTENTS

INTRODUCTION

A prevailing fallacy among some observers of Communist Bloc states is that these systems are both monolithic and static. Such an oversimplification of the intricacy and complexity of communist societies can lead to unfortunate and misleading results, whether reflected in policy decisions or in research designs. The extreme form of this view suggests that by knowing Marxism-Leninism alone the scholar is well enough equipped to understand the subtle workings of communist-based systems. Indeed, it can be argued, and it seems effectively, that such a position unavoidably leads to distortions and misinterpretations of how any *particular* communist system works. In contrast to this view, the underlying assumption of this study is that socialist or communist societies (just as other types of systems) are intrinsically dynamic rather than static. Existing communist regimes (and among them the Yugoslav) respond to practical demands emanating from their environments in much the same way as do other states. Furthermore, as will be demonstrated in the course of this monograph, the specific *variety* of communist-type system developed is in large measure precisely an adaptation to such practical concerns. Our task, therefore, is to observe such adaptations and, specifically, to detect and measure their impact within the context of the Yugoslav experience.

The basic procedure for research and analysis has required setting up selected check-points along the path of Yugoslav state development. The strategy has thus called for a discussion of the interwar Yugoslav environment as a backdrop against which subsequent changes in the system can be illuminated. As the analysis will demonstrate, although the entry of Yugoslavia into its communist stage has meant the introduction of new institutional forms, a legacy of prior experience with sociopolitical order has also conditioned the concrete expression of these institutions. Furthermore, the communist phase of Yugoslav state development is quite clearly neither homogeneous nor undifferentiated over time; it has been a major task of this study to detect and to elaborate the salient phases of the transformation of Yugoslav society within its over-all communist stage. Accordingly, both the analysis and the discussion will center around these periods of Yugoslav socialist development: the push for intensive communist growth (the "administrative period"), the reaction against Soviet "state capitalism" and a resulting modification (and relaxation) of institutions, the consolidation of the "Yugoslav road" with relative stabilization of new institutional forms, and the promise of even further liberalization that emanates from more recent economic reforms and changes in political leadership. Each of these phases of growth and modification in Yugoslav socialism is reflected in (and discussed in terms of) both the ideology or belief structure and the institutions of the society. Furthermore, the over-all analysis will show that the shifting patterns of Yugoslav associations with other states and, specifically, its changing relations with Soviet and Western Bloc countries are also reflected in the dynamics of internal sociopolitical forms and experience.

This study and analysis of Yugoslav development will yield a basic description of general trends over time; as such, it will permit statements about relevant modifications in the Yugoslav system since its foundation as a communist party state. However, the study should also be instructive as regards more basic observations about how socialist or communist systems are transformed generally, in addition to tentative prognostications about how these systems might develop in the future given the growth of proper conditions in the communist world. As will be seen, the lessons taught by the wielding of governmental power, as well as pressures from the constellation of forces that affect world affairs, have had their impact upon the development of the Yugoslav brand of socialism.

Any study such as this unavoidably owes a debt of gratitude to many people. First and foremost, the author would like to express his thanks to Wayne S. Vucinich, not only for his counsel and constructive criticism in relation to this particular work, but also for his guidance, encouragement, and selfless help over the course of several years. Secondly, this study would have been impossible without the dedicated assistance of two individuals—Bogdan Denitch and Paul Sjeklocha —both of whom did much of the yeoman work in gathering the basic data. And finally, numerous other but unnamed individuals have through informal discussions and debate contributed much to the value of this study.

The author would like to offer special thanks to A. Dean McKenzie for drawing the map of Yugoslavia.

M. GEORGE ZANINOVICH

Department of Political Science
University of Oregon

Pronunciation Guide

A number of symbols or letters (and combinations of letters) peculiar to the Latin version of Serbo-Croatian may be unfamiliar to the English reader. The following represents a brief enumeration and explanation of these symbols relating to names of places, names of persons, and other Serbo-Croatian words found in both the text and the footnotes of this monograph.

Serbo-Croatian	*English Phonetic Rendering*	*Example*
c	ts (ca*ts*)	Stepinac
č	ch (*ch*eap)	Maček
ć	tch (i*tch*)	Ranković
dj	j (*J*erry)	Djilas
dž	dge (e*dge*)	Hadžistević
i	e (sh*e*)	Tito
j	y (*y*es)	Jugoslavija
lj	llio (mi*lli*on)	Ljubljana
nj	gn (*gn*u)	Njegoš
š	sh (*sh*ed)	Nikšić
ž	zh (plea*s*ure)	Žabljak

The Federal People's Republic of Yugoslavia
Federativna Narodna Republika Jugoslavija

Area: 98,766 square miles (255,804 sq. km.)
Population: 19,755,000 (1966)
Communist Party membership: 1,046,018 (1966)

Major cities:	Population (1961)
Belgrade	587,900
Zagreb	427,320
Skopje	162,000
Sarajevo	142,420
Ljubljana	133,390
Novi Sad	102,390
Rijeka	100,340

Birth rate: 20.2 per 1,000 (1966)
Death rate: 8.0 per 1,000 (1966)
Natural increase: 12.2 per 1,000 (1966)
Marriages: 8.5 per 1,000 (1966)
Emigration: 10,583 (1966)
Literacy (10 years and older): 80.3 (1961)

Economic indices for 1965 (1952=100)

National income	301
Mining and industry	455
Agriculture	211
Trade and commerce	339
New construction	694
Catering and tourism	934
Living costs	281
Private income	545
Imports	293
Exports	388
Trade balance (export/import)	85

Transportation and communication	*1957*	*1965*
Travel by individuals—rail	170,951	236,033
Travel by individuals—air	52,835	479,701
Number of passenger cars	21,570	187,842
TV receivers (individuals per receiver)	149*	25*
Railway movement (1000 kms)	137,765	179,076
Telephones in use	198,055	414,656
Communication service index (1956=100)	110	231

*These figures are based upon data for 1962 and 1966.

AUSTRIA

HUNGARY

ITALY

RUMANIA

LJUBLJANA
SLOVENIA
ZAGREB
CROATIA
RIJEKA

VOJVODINA
NOVI SAD

SERBIA

BEOGRAD

BOSNIA
&
HERCEGOVINA
SARAJEVO

SPLIT

NIS

BULGARIA

MONTE-
NEGRO

PRISTINA

KOSMET

DUBROVNIK
TITOGRAD

SKOPLJE

ALBANIA

MACEDONIA

GREECE

KEY

Boundaries

COUNTRY   — — —

REPUBLIC   — · — · —

AUTONOMOUS
REGION ···········

Cities   ●

Capitals o

The Development of Socialist Yugoslavia

1. THE PHYSICAL-ECOLOGICAL SETTING

Often neglected in the analysis of state development is the impact of certain physical factors that contribute to the historical experience of a people and that, therefore, also affect the articulation of a people's institutional life. These environmental factors (for example, the rigors of the Karst) have played an important role in determining the basic modes of economy developed in the South Slavic region; this, in turn, cannot but have its effect upon the nature of emerging sociopolitical institutions and instruments of control.[1] In addition, the historical experience of the Yugoslav people, situated on the frontier that separates the Crescent from the Cross and thus serving as Europe's human barricade against the onslaught of the Turk, has also had its impact. Finally, we must point to the South Slavic position on one of the primary trading routes of the ancient era—namely, the Morava-Vardar Valley—which even in modern times was to entice the

[1]For a fine over-all description of the physical and ecological setting of Yugoslavia, see: Anton Melik, *Jugoslavija—zemljepisni pregled (Yugoslavia—Geographical Survey)* (Ljubljana: Državna založba Slovenije, 1958). A good brief general history is provided by Muriel Heppell and Frank B. Singleton in: *Yugoslavia* (New York: Frederick A. Praeger, 1964).

German expansionist. As we shall see, governments in power must unavoidably come to grips with problems arising from the physical-ecological situation of a nation state.

The complex ethnic composition of the Balkan peninsula places the Yugoslavs within a larger sea of diverse peoples and cultures. Understandably, therefore, several foreign states with different languages and religious expression, in addition to varied historical experiences, border upon Yugoslavia. At the present, the longest Yugoslav land boundary is with Hungary (623 km.), followed by Rumania (557), Bulgaria (536), Albania (465), Austria (324), Greece (262), and Italy (202).[2] Except for the Italian-Yugoslav frontier and the fluctuations that occurred during World War II, these borders have not changed since the first Yugoslav state was established at the conclusion of World War I. As a result of historical, ethnic, and ideological forces, Yugoslav relations with these countries have vacillated from normal and friendly to hostile and bellicose. The total land boundary of Yugoslavia, most of which touches upon other socialist or communist states, is 2,969 kilometers; the Adriatic coastline with its many islands extends some 2,092 kilometers along the western boundary.[3] Present-day conflicts that involve Yugoslavia, as well as its political participation within supranational units, can be understood largely in terms of its physical location at the crossroads between East and West.

The Yugoslav nation is situated in an area of Europe that has long been prominent in the history of man; it

[2]Vladimir Blašković, *Ekonomska geografija Jugoslavije (Economic Geography of Yugoslavia)* (Zagreb: Birozavod, 1962), p. 45.

[3]*Ibid.*, p. 33.

has both suffered the ravages and reaped the benefits of Western as well as Eastern civilizations. Various parts of the country, especially the Dalmatian coast, had been colonized and influenced by the early Greeks. Furthermore, nearly all of present-day Yugoslavia was for some time incorporated into and developed by the Roman Empire. With the splitting up of a weakened Roman Empire, the line between East and West became firmly and tragically etched upon South Slavic lands. Today the imprint of Byzantium is most apparent in Serbia and Macedonia (the Yugoslav "East"), whereas that of Rome is clearly visible in the cultural expression of Croatia and Slovenia (the Yugoslav "West"). A mosaic of early and primitive peoples (Illyrians, Celts, Greeks, Romans, Goths, Huns, Avars, Slavs, Mongols, and so forth) invaded, ravaged, settled, civilized, and perished in what is presently the territory of Yugoslavia.[4] Much of the country was under Turkish Ottoman rule either permanently or sporadically from the end of the fourteenth century until the "sick man of Europe" was finally dismembered at the conclusion of World War I. Each people who lived in and ruled over South Slavic lands left traces of its civilization—its language, its cultural forms, and its habits. The people who occupied the region the longest, and held it the most firmly, of course left the most lasting imprint upon the land and its history. The process of ethnogenesis, a fusion of various invading tribes with indigenous elements and

[4]For early Slavic migration and history, see: Samuel H. Cross, *Slavic Civilization Through the Ages* (Cambridge: Harvard University Press, 1948); Karl H. Menges, *An Outline of the Early History of the Slavs* (New York: Columbia University Press, 1953); and Francis Dvornik, *The Slavs: Their Early History and Civilization* (Boston: American Academy of Arts and Sciences, 1956).

their consequent Slavicization, in addition to the homogenization of the South Slavs, although fascinating, are factors too complex to pursue at any length here. We need only note the vivid survivals and residuals of early non-Slavic tribal and patriarchal systems, the transformation of Romanized Illyrian tribes into South Slavic peoples, and the emergence of new ethnic groups under Turkish Ottoman rule—to illustrate the complexity of the problem. The interplay of these conflicting forces gave rise to the final ethnic and cultural conglomerate that constitutes the Yugoslav peoples today.

Being diversified in population and culture and strategically located, Yugoslavia has presented an easy target for foreign pressures and intrigue. This problem has also been reflected in the complexity of ideological expression and national identification in Yugoslavia. As a result, in modern times disgruntled minority elements, embedded in the Yugoslav ethnic conglomerate, have been used as a means by which foreign governments have justified intervention. External pressures, therefore, have clearly been an important factor in the development of Yugoslav foreign and domestic policies. For example, German hegemony in Europe had a profound effect upon the country's internal life in the 1930's, not the least of which was the tightening of controls by the then existing regime. Similarly, the ascendancy of the Soviet Union since 1945 as the dominant force in Eastern Europe has greatly affected the development of Yugoslav foreign and domestic policies.

Furthermore, the Yugoslav position astride one of the major European communication and transportation lines could not but affect its economic and political life. The principal railway between the Middle East and Western Europe—the famed Orient Express—

traverses Yugoslav territory. Similarly, the primary connection between rich Central European economies and Adriatic and Mediterranean ports (Rijeka, Salonika, and so on) lies across Yugoslav lands. Finally, the Danube, which is one of the major commercial waterways of Europe, winds its way through Yugoslavia toward its outlet on the Black Sea. Understandably, therefore, any international commission that purports to control navigation on the Danube is of vital concern to the Yugoslav state. In a Europe politically divided the Danube unavoidably involves Yugoslavia in power squabbles that may not always coincide with the country's best interest. Although the bulk of Yugoslav trade has been and continues to be with the West, the Danube today is controlled by states strongly predisposed toward a Soviet orientation. The result has been that Yugoslavia has and is now developing its Adriatic littoral as a commercial outlet to the world.

Internal Yugoslav physiography can most appropriately be described as harsh and challenging. Most of present-day Yugoslavia is of a mountainous character, or at best of a rolling-hill sort of terrain. Only in the extreme northern sectors of the country does one find extensive low-lying and open country fully compatible with modern technical agricultural economy. These northern regions (that is, the Vojvodina and Slavonia) constitute the Yugoslav share of the vast and fertile Pannonian Plain of East Central Europe. Taken as a whole, we find that only 29.4 per cent of Yugoslav territory lies below 200 meters; on the other hand, 45.2 per cent is found at an altitude of 500 meters or greater.[5] The major portions of the high country in

---

[5]Blašković, *Economic Geography of Yugoslavia*, p. 45.

Yugoslavia include the Julian and Dinaric Alps, and the Shar, Rhodope, and Carpatho-Balkan mountains. The Dinaric Karst region paralleling the Adriatic is of special concern because of a soluble limestone composition that makes soil formation and hence agriculture difficult indeed.

The over-all rugged internal physiography of Yugoslavia would of course have its impact upon the history as well as the traditions of the people. As a matter of fact, many observers attribute a measure of partisan success (as well as a stubborn posture in the face of great adversity) during World War II to the difficulty and ruggedness of Yugoslav terrain. In point of fact, Yugoslav topography with its difficult accessibility proved a formidable obstacle to mechanized German armies and, thus, provided ideal conditions for guerrilla activities. The mountainous character of Yugoslavia also contributed to the abandonment (or, at least, indefinite postponement) of agricultural collectivization and has hampered the introduction of mechanized techniques as requisites for effective collective farming operations. The Julian-Dinaric high alpine chain effectively cuts off the interior and more fertile regions of Yugoslavia (that is, the Sava and Morava valleys, Slavonia, and the Vojvodina) from easy and direct access to the sea and thus to world trade. Accordingly, in one sense the Danube provides the logical "outlet to the sea" *via* the Black Sea and the Dardanelles and, as indicated above, therefore becomes of crucial importance for foreign commerce. Direct access to the Mediterranean Sea from the Pannonian region can also be had by way of the old Morava-Vardar trade route and the Greek-controlled Aegean port of Salonika. In view of problems deriving from these foreign-controlled routes to the sea and ports, the Yugoslav state has developed Rijeka as a major Adriatic port and has improved transport routes through Slovenia. Current Yugoslav plans stress the need to construct even better access routes to Rijeka and to develop further the commercial potential of the Adriatic.

Needless to say, special geographic and historical conditions in Yugoslavia have been responsible for its mosaic of subcultures and thus for many of its problems. Its strategic location more than once invited hordes and armies that overran the countryside and superimposed yet other strata of culture and history. The location of the Balkans at the gateway to the wealth and grandeur of Near Eastern civilizations has of course contributed toward this appeal to invading peoples.

2: THE YUGOSLAV SYSTEM IN THE PRE-ENTRY STAGE

Demographic Structure

The structure of Yugoslav population has changed rather significantly over the past fifty years. From a backward and exclusively rural countryside in the early part of the century, Yugoslavia has developed a significant measure of industrial capability. Along with this, we find the demographic effects of movement from village to city and the rise of managerial and professional classes with the usual vested interests. Furthermore, we discover a general expansion of contacts with foreign states (both East and West) as well as the development of consumer tastes.

Just prior to Yugoslav involvement in World War II its population in 1939 stood at the 15,596,000 figure. This indicated a population increase of more than 4,000,000 since 1918 and the founding of the first Yugoslav state.[1] In this early period, the centers of

[1] Savezni zavod za statistiku (Federal Bureau of Statistics), *Statistički godišnjak FNRJ, 1955 (Statistical Yearbook FPRY, 1955)* (Beograd, 1955), p. 54. These census figures include only the territory that comprised the then existing Yugoslavia; they do not include additional territory acquired after the census was taken.

population were primarily in the northern and north-western regions of the country—the Vojvodina, Serbia proper, Croatia, and Slovenia; these were also the most advanced regions industrially, culturally, and technologically. Cultural and political life in the young nation was dominated by urban centers such as Belgrade with 266,849 inhabitants, Zagreb with 185,581, Subotica with 100,058 and Ljubljana with 79,056—all based upon the 1931 census.[2] Densely populated regions were also to be found in the highly developed agricultural sectors of the North and, especially, in the Vojvodina and the Sava and Morava valleys. An extremely high birth rate coupled with high infant mortality were to be found in the southern areas of Yugoslavia, particularly in Kosovo-Metohija and in Macedonia, regions that were also the least advanced in culture, technology, and economy. Southern Yugoslavia could be characterized generally as having a diffuse population scattered in small villages through mountainous and rather inaccessible terrain. In addition to the urban centers of the North, the largely rural Kosovo-Metohija and Macedonia showed high population density, which could be explained mainly by the high birth rate of the indigenous Albanians. Generally, the less developed and more diffuse southern regions lacked the large, Western-oriented urban concentrations found in the northern part of Yugoslavia. Between the wars the over-all trend in Yugoslavia indicated a decrease in both infant mortality and general death rates.[3] This of course suggests the effects of some degree of modernization coupled with more advanced medical facilities.

[2]Kraljevina Jugoslavija (Kingdom of Yugoslavia), *Statistički godišnjak, 1936 (Statistical Yearbook, 1936)* (Beograd: Štamparija "Janićević," 1937), VII, 62–63.

[3]*Statistical Yearbook, 1938–39*, IX, 114–15, 122.

Yugoslavia could be viewed (although less dramatically) as a sort of Soviet Union in miniature because of its ethnic, linguistic, and religious diversity. The principal ethnic and national groups within Yugoslavia include Serbs, Croats, Slovenes, Macedonians, and Montenegrins—all belonging to the South Slavic linguistic group (see Table 1). The Serbian (including Montenegrin) and Croatian languages, designated jointly as Serbo-Croatian, are essentially similar and, considered together, represent the official language of the state. The primary distinction between the two stems from the use of two different alphabets and somewhat different exposure to foreign influences. The Serbs, who accepted Christianity from the East, employ a Greek-based alphabet, the *ćirilica*; on the other hand, the Croats use a Latin script (that is, *latinica*), since they took their religious instruction from the West. A widespread interwar feeling was that the Serbs and Croats represented two distinct ethnic groups, each of which possessed its own history and traditions.

According to the 1931 census, the combined Serb and Croat ethnic element accounted for about 10,731,000 persons and 77 per cent of the total population.[4] However, the generally agreed-upon ambiguity of this 1931 census, in conjunction with a state policy designed to discourage separate ethnic awareness, makes it difficult to determine clearly the number of ethnic Serbs as opposed to Croats for the interwar period. Suffice it to say that those who considered themselves Serbs as opposed to Croats were somewhat greater in number.

[4]The figure quoted here includes Macedonians, Montenegrins, Bulgars, and "undeclared" as Serbo-Croats, since the 1931 census had failed to distinguish these as separate Slavic ethnic elements. George W. Hoffman and Fred W. Neal, *Yugoslavia and the New Communism* (New York: Twentieth Century Fund, 1962), p. 29.

The Slovenes, who speak a distinct Slavic language, numbered about 1,135,000 according to the 1931 census. Their position on the alpine slopes of northwest Yugoslavia understandably resulted in cultural forms that mirror strong Germanic or Romanic elements depending upon the locality. Inadequate census-taking between the wars also makes it difficult to estimate the exact number of Montenegrins and Macedonians (who also speak a distinct Slavic language) for the pre-entry stage. Both groups were included within the general ethnic category of Serbo-Croat for census purposes by the Yugoslav interwar regime. However, if we project backward from the 1948 census,[5] we might estimate 700,000 Macedonians and 380,000 Montenegrins for the early 1930 period.

Of the numerous minority ethnic groups in Yugoslavia three have been of major significance—namely, the Albanian, the German, and the Magyar. The largest non-Slavic ethnic minority in Yugoslavia has been and remains today the so-called *Šiptari* or Albanian. The 1931 census placed the Yugoslav Albanian population at 505,000, most of whom lived under trying and meager circumstances; they predominated in the Kosovo-Metohija region of southern Serbia and in the western areas of Macedonia.[6] Overwhelmingly Moslem, the Albanians of Yugoslavia speak a distinct Indo-European language, which some linguists recognize as deriving historically from ancient Thraco-Illyrian. Following close upon the Albanian population, the German ethnic minority in Yugoslavia numbered about half a million according to the 1931 census. This

[5]*Statistical Yearbook FPRY, 1962,* p. 308.
[6]Hoffman and Neal, *Yugoslavia and the New Communism,* p. 29.

German element was centered for the most part in the fertile Vojvodina and tended to dominate the over-all commercial and business activity in that region. Finally, the Magyars, who were 468,000 strong in Yugoslavia in 1931, represented the third largest non-Slavic minority. They lived and worked primarily in Slavonia and Vojvodina, regions adjoining southern Hungary, where they formed a large part of the peasant and artisan class. Other ethnic groups of some importance and size include Turks, Rumanians, Gypsies, Slovaks, and Czechs. Understandably, such minority ethnic groups as existed provided fertile ground for generating tension between Yugoslavia and its more ambitious neighbors.

Classifying a population by religion is indeed a difficult task, for there are obviously degrees of religious practice and identification (see Table 3). Based upon 1931 figures, about 6,784,000 persons were designated as Orthodox Christians, which also represented about 48.7 per cent of the population.[7] Ethnically, this included Serbs, Montenegrins, and Macedonians, in addition to Russian, Bulgarian, and Rumanian minority elements. Lacking an effective international affiliation, and with its own autocephalous ecclesiastical administration, the Orthodox Church has relied historically upon the regime in power for both support and sustenance. The Orthodox faithful predominated in the eastern reaches of Yugoslavia and, primarily, in Serbia, Montenegro, and Macedonia. However, in the heavily Catholic western regions sporadic but compact Orthodox communities could also be found. The second

[7]Ljubiša Stojković and Miloš Martić, *National Minorities in Yugoslavia* (Belgrade: Publishing and Editing Enterprise "Yugoslavia," 1952), pp. 30–31.

largest religious group in Yugoslavia were the Roman Catholics, who in 1931 numbered 5,217,000 and represented about 37.4 per cent of the over-all population. The Croat and Slovene ethnic groups formed the bulk of the Roman Catholic constituency in Yugoslavia and were generally predominant in the western sections of the country. Because of its organizational ties with the Vatican, as well as effective administrative and educational institutions, the Catholic Church in Yugoslavia was able to remain vital and dynamic. This religious division has also been instrumental in deepening the rift between Serb and Croat, an ethnic distribution that tends to be viewed largely in religious terms.

We also find in interwar Yugoslavia about two million persons of the Moslem religious confession. Most of these appeared to be Islamicized ethnic Slavs, a considerable portion of them Albanian speakers, and a relatively small number of them Turks. The great majority of Islamicized Slavs were situated in the province of Bosnia-Hercegovina; the language spoken by them could not be easily distinguished from Serbo-Croatian. Since religion has traditionally governed social and moral life among Moslems, a number of Turkish words have been incorporated into the speech of these Islamicized Slavs. Being somewhat less aware of their Slavic origins than the Serb or Croat, these Moslem Slavs have tended to displace nationality with religion as the more generic identity, which was especially the case until after World War I. The Moslem population taken as a whole (that is, Slav, Albanian, and Turk) lived primarily in Macedonia, Kosovo-Metohija, and Bosnia-Hercegovina. Although ethnically divided, they have been homogeneous in that all Yugoslav Moslems belong to the Sunni confession.

In the pre-entry stage demographic-based conflict variables (that is, Serb against Croat, village against city, Orthodox against Catholic) contributed significantly to the instability of the Yugoslav system. The young, inexperienced state found it difficult to reconcile the contradictory demands made upon it by the various competing ethnic and religious groups. The response of the interwar regime was to consolidate and centralize power in order to contain these divisive forces. No tradition of compromise and accommodation of differences had been bequeathed to the struggling interwar Yugoslav system. Accordingly, easy solutions to conflict were sought through power; the result was the demise of the young Balkan state.

Political Beliefs and Movements

The pattern of beliefs in Yugoslavia, articulated by various parties and movements, had their basis in the ethnic and religious division indicated above. These ethnic differences ultimately degenerated into vicious struggles between groups who placed "blood relations" and localism higher than democratic form on their respective value scales. Such an inadequate value consensus meant that, although it might have constituted a government, Yugoslavia between the wars could by no means be considered a nation state.[8] The government held a monopoly over instruments of force, but it lacked the authority and confidence necessary to achieve co-operation without force. This can be ex-

[8]For a good interwar political history see: Ferdo Čulinović, *Jugoslavija izmedju dva rata (Yugoslavia Between the Two Wars)* (Zagreb: Jugoslovenska akademija znanosti i umjetnosti, 1961).

plained in large part by the absence of a yet fully effective "Yugoslav Idea," in addition to the lack of other experiences and values that could serve as a matrix for voluntary co-operative effort.

We have already seen that the Serbs and the Croats felt that they possessed separate if not incompatible traditions and values.[9] This sense of distinct history and tradition, coupled with religious and cultural differences, provided the ground for chauvinistic appeals and political movements for, on the one hand, domination by the Serb because of his political successes or, on the other, separatism for or domination by the Croat because of his advanced culture. In particular, we find that one ethnic group (that is, the Serbs) was *perceived as* attempting to dominate the system completely and, by so doing, to exploit other ethnic groups within the young state. Other ethnic and cultural forces in Yugoslavia were not quite so deeply concerned with or capable of asserting themselves. For example, the Slovenes, who spent a millennium under foreign rule, appear to have been considerably less intense nationalists than either the Serb or the Croat. On the other hand, the Montenegrins have always been very proud of their independent history as well as their distinct traditions, and thus they displayed a well-developed sense of nation group solidarity. This holds true despite a language spoken in Montenegro not easily distinguishable from Serbian. For the Macedonians the idea of a distinct Macedonian-Slav ethnic and historical

[9]For literary discussions that capture the mood and character of the South Slavs, in addition to the nature and intensity of Serb-Croat differences, see: Rebecca West, *Black Lamb and Grey Falcon* (New York: The Viking Press, 1940); and Louis Adamic, *My Native Land* (New York and London: Harper and Bros., 1943).

entity is very largely a post-World War II contrivance and development. Before World War II, most of the people of Macedonia usually thought of themselves as either Serbs, Albanians, Turks, Greeks, or Bulgars. Relatively few, and then only the more radical elements, apparently considered themselves to be Macedonians as such.

Prior to World War I, we also tend to find a similar phenomenon among the Moslem Slavs—namely, a lack of strong national identity. As a result, their religious commitment seemed to take precedence over and to obscure their historical origins. However, between the wars a stronger, more vocal sense of nation group solidarity was developed among Slavic-speaking Moslems in Yugoslavia. This raised a new problem: if these Moslems were to be considered South Slavs, were they to be classified as Serbs or Croats? Furthermore, were they to be identified historically with the Serbian or the Croatian experience and traditions? Understandably, both the extreme Serb and the Croat nationalist claimed the Moslem Slav as his ethnic brother, with some of these Moslem Slavs responding also by a close identification with one of these groups. However, the bulk of the Moslems, as a result of this uncertainty, were guided by political opportunism in their relations with both Serbs and Croats—that is, they displayed a tendency to cater to ethnic elements currently in positions of power. Another important result was that Moslem Slavs proclaimed themselves as "genuine Yugoslavs" in order to avoid commitment to either group.

From these developments, we can see that the absence of shared historical experience was crucial for the Yugoslav belief system. The various ethnic groups in Yugoslavia could hardly identify with and share (both emotionally and psychologically) the Serbian historical and revolutionary tradition. Accordingly, the Slovene and Croat found little reason to revere *Kosovo Polje,* the great Serbian defeat at the hands of the Turk, as a truly "Yugoslav" epic tragedy; neither could they identify closely with the Serbian revolutionary tradition of the nineteenth century. Yet the problem of transforming uniquely Serbian hero myths and epics into genuinely Yugoslav ones was crucial for the authority structure of the new state. Since it failed in this attempt, the regime was understandably weakened and ultimately destined for collapse. What was needed was a new historical experience, a new political founding shared by all, which might create a more unified system of beliefs. Serbian and Croatian hero myths and epics would have to be replaced by uniquely Yugoslav ones as the new basis of authority. In addition, the "positive" heritage of all ethnic groups in this way might be identified as a common possession of all Yugoslavs.

Earlier and, specifically, prior to World War I, Serbia has been oriented in cultural and educational matters toward France and Russia. Furthermore, most of the civil servants and intellectuals in the new Yugoslavia were educated in France prior to the war. In fact, close political as well as cultural ties inaugurated between France and Serbia before World War I continued until the late 1930's; therefore, the French impact upon the course of events in the new state was significant. In addition, the second language in Serbia was French, whereas for Croatia, Slovenia, and the Vojvodina it tended to be German. The two major universities (Belgrade and Zagreb) also reflected this division since they were largely organized on the basis of French and German models respectively. This tendency to identify with the French as opposed to the German tradition further magnified the separatist feelings of the Serb and Croat.

Most major political movements already had a history prior to World War I in what was to become Yugoslav territory after Versailles. Accordingly, political ideologies had been developed within the context of multinational, imperial systems prior to the existence of the Yugoslav state, or within an independent nation state such as Serbia. The various parties and their beliefs were thus primarily a function of ethnic rather than of class solidarity; party affiliation was determined primarily by blood and ethnic localisms and only secondarily by interest. Until late in the 1930's when a United Opposition movement to the Regency was formed, most of the major parties were generally skeptical about the so-called utopian "Yugoslav Idea." And those who did favor it usually saw it in terms of either a "Greater Serbian" or a "Greater Croatian" state. Upon its creation, the United Opposition sought a solution to the Serb-Croat rift within a framework permitting autonomy of "national entities," a policy eventually given partial effect in the 1939 *sporazum* or agreement between Serb and Croat leaders. Included among the more viable political movements and parties were: the Croat Peasant Party (led by Radić); the Serb Democratic Party; the Serb Radicals (led by Pašić); the Slovene People's Party; and the Communist Party.[10] The Moslem Party affords a special case in that it was

[10]The role of interwar Yugoslav parties is discussed by Carlo Sforza in: *Fifty Years of War and Diplomacy in the Balkans* (New York: Columbia University Press, 1940); and, Ivan Avakumovic, *History of the Communist Party of Yugoslavia* (Aberdeen: Aberdeen University Press, 1964).

largely a movement defending the parochial interests of landlords facing the threat of reform. To these must be added various jingoistic movements as, for example, the fascist Ustaši of Pavelić. The popular-based parties were mainly peasant movements concerned with the problem of adapting a peasant society to an age of technology. In conjunction with this, we find that in Serbia most officials were at most one generation removed from local village culture and traditions. Not surprisingly, therefore, an ideology emerged that stressed a sort of primitive egalitarianism as well as a "rugged" peasant individualism. Coupled with this, we find a chronic distrust on the part of the peasant of things that emanate from the official central authority, which of course compounded the problems of administration and social order. As a result, a major issue that confronted interwar Yugoslav politics was precisely how to effectively integrate the peasant into the social and economic system.

The special character of interwar Yugoslav politics was found in the absence of any effective cross-ethnic or national party. Accordingly, the Serb peasantry was inclined to distrust the Croat peasant far more perhaps than he would his own Serb bourgeoisie; in short, historical and ethnic ties seemed to take precedence over class identification. A noteworthy exception to this was the Communist Party, which attempted (but without success) to develop a country-wide movement based upon its customary class appeal. However, we find that even the Communist Party was organized until 1938 along ethnic or regional lines as a result of Yugoslav environmental heterogeneity.[11] Given these largely eth-

[11]Vladimir Dedijer, *Tito* (New York: Simon and Schuster, 1953), pp. 115–18.

nically based movements, the problem of keeping tensions and emotions at a low level, in addition to maintaining orderly change, understandably became quite difficult. As a result, the cement that held the Yugoslav system together was comprised of the army, the police, and the bureaucracy; the government relied upon instruments of force rather than upon an articulated shared belief system or a developed sense of nationhood. Even many of the small businessmen or petty bourgeoisie were alienated and became "anti-Yugoslav" in sentiment; this was due largely to a state policy that cut off old Austro-Hungarian provincial markets and opened up the country to foreign (mainly French) capital. Accordingly, we find that the Croat (or Serb) separatist movement was backed by most segments of territorial Croatia (or Serbia) irrespective of class identification.

The Kingdom of Serbs, Croats, and Slovenes began as a deeply divided country with sharply divergent cultural traditions and with political factions ready to use appeals that intensified these differences.[12] The major conflict-point involved the clash between old, established Serbian power centers and new constituencies that earlier had been under the Austro-Hungarian regime. For most Serbian intellectuals and politicians throughout this interwar period, the role that Serbia had played in and immediately prior to World War I was viewed as crucial and historic. It was difficult for the Serbs to set aside a sense of national pride that had been won by the blood of revolution and war. The "Yugoslav Idea," therefore, was unavoidably destined

[12]For insightful analyses of these problems, see: West, *Black Lamb and Grey Falcon,* pp. 588–629; and Adamic, *My Native Land,* pp. 310–26.

to suffer while the Serbs and the Croats busied themselves learning something about politics.

The Sociopolitical System

The Kingdom of Serbs, Croats, and Slovenes was theoretically conceived as a partnership of South Slavic peoples. Despite formal recognition of various ethnic groups and religious confessions, the practical operation of Yugoslav politics and government created hostility and distrust among nearly all factions. Crucial perhaps was that those institutions that had existed prior to World War I were Serbian, the remaining political forces having been under foreign rule and occupation. This had two effects: first, it gave the Serbs an advantage in that Yugoslav institutions were little more than transformed Serbian ones; and, second, it gave dissident forces some cause for alleging that they were in effect merely second-class citizens within a "Greater Serbia." In addition, it became immediately apparent that some of the new structures of authority were in conflict with traditional Slavic institutions.

As so many traditional forms in Yugoslavia, the extended family or *zadruga* had begun to disintegrate as the basis for social order since the beginning of the nineteenth century.[13] Certain instruments (including voluntary co-operatives) linked to peasant parties were introduced as substitutes for creating a basis of order and integration in the villages. Since the French ad-

---

[13]For problems relating to agriculture and the peasantry, see: Mijo Mirković, *Ekonomska historija Jugoslavije (Economic History of Yugoslavia)* (Zagreb: Ekonomski pregled, 1958); and Jozo Tomasevich, *Peasants, Politics and Economic Change in Yugoslavia* (Stanford, Calif.: Stanford University Press, 1955).

ministrative system functioned as the model, the local prefects in Yugoslavia were appointed by the central authority; these in turn appointed the lower-ranking officials and local councils. Understandably, therefore, hostility and conflict ensued between "outside" administrative forces and the traditional leaders and customs of the village; the perception of the environment by the peasantry caused unending strife between them and a hostile, unfeeling, and remote central power. This was true even in Serbia itself where the peasantry had played an important role in the government between 1901 and 1912.[14] In violation of this experience, however, the new Yugoslav state adopted both a civil service structure and a police system based upon an alien Austro-Hungarian model.

The constitution of the new state, designated the Vidovdan Constitution, was in large measure based upon a 1903 Serbian document.[15] It was a "liberal" constitution in the sense of extending suffrage to all sectors and factions in society and supporting social legislation. On the other hand, it appeared to be "undemocratic" in matters relating to the scope of state police power over the regulation of free speech and assembly. The result was that for all practical purposes the authority of the central government remained limitless and unencumbered.

[14]The nature and structure of Serbian parties before World War I is examined by Wayne S. Vucinich in: *Serbia Between East and West; The Events of 1903–1908* (Stanford, Calif.: Stanford University Press, 1954).

[15]"Ustav Kraljevine Srba, Hrvata i Slovenaca od 28 Juna 1921" ("Constitution of the Kingdom of Serbs, Croats, and Slovenes of 28 June 1921"), *Službene novine Kraljevine Srba, Hrvata, i Slovenaca (Official Journal of the Kingdom of Serbs, Croats, and Slovenes)*, II, 142-A (June 28, 1921), 1–6.

Let us turn briefly to an examination of the strength of the various parties as constituted in the Yugoslav *skupština* or assembly. In 1920 we find these election results: Serb Radicals 98, Serb Democrats 94, Croat Peasants 49, Slovene People's Party 27, Moslems 24, Serb Agrarians 39, Communists 58, Social Democrats 10, and Republicans 4. Here we must note that the Democrats represented a shaky and temporary coalition of groups, a coalition that was soon to lose most of its strength. One factor contributing to the large communist vote was that many ethnic minorities were forbidden their own parties; therefore, for many it meant choosing between Serb or Croat parties *or* a Communist Party that appeared to have little ethnic affiliation.[16] To this must also be added such factors as war disillusionment, a historic pro-Russian sentiment, and class identification as explaining the large communist vote. Nonetheless, the basic ruling coalition remained stable until 1926 and the death of Pašić, at which point the fragmentation and weakening of the Serb parties intensified. Usually this coalition consisted of the Serb Radicals, the Slovene People's Party, the Moslems, and one additional Serb party.

As early as 1922, however, significant shifts in the voting pattern were already evident. The Croat Peasant Party managed to strengthen its contingent by electing 70 delegates, whereas the Serb Democrats, who had favored a degree of Croatian autonomy, lost some of their support to the Pašić Radical Party. Another factor contributing to this redistribution of power in the early 1920's was of course the outlawing of the Com-

[16]Hugh Seton-Watson, *The East European Revolution* (New York: Frederick A. Praeger, 1962), pp. 27–28, 35–36, 40–41.

munist Party.[17] The cabinets tended to remain stable, except that control of the ministry moved from the Serb Democrats of Davidović to the Pašić Radicals. Furthermore, as a result of its increased strength the Croat Peasant Party was able to participate in the 1926 government. This general stability, however, was only apparent and short-lived, and merely hid deep-seated hostilities.

The assassination of the leader of the Croat Peasant Party, Stjepan Radić, opened a new phase in Yugoslav politics. Vladimir Maček, the new head of the Croat Peasant Party, publicly endorsed Radić's declaration that the murders of June, 1928, "have wiped out the constitution; there is nothing left except the King and

[17]The new Yugoslav Royal Government outlawed the Communist Party of Yugoslavia on December 19, 1920, by a cabinet decree known as the "Obznana" (Notification), which banned all its activities and propaganda. The author of "Obznana" was the Minister of Interior Milorad Drašković, who, it is alleged, paid for the authorship with his life. In retaliation the National Assembly passed the Law on the Protection of Public Safety and Order in the State (August 2, 1921) throwing the communist deputies out of the Assembly and providing special measures to deal with all activities and propaganda against the state. Julijana Vržinić, *Kraljevina Srba, Hrvata i Slovenaca do Vidovdanskog procesa (The Kingdom of Serbs, Croats, and Slovenes up to Vidovdan's Law)* (Beograd: Rad, 1956), p. 109; "Zakon Kraljevine Srba, Hrvata i Slovenaca o zaštiti javne bezbednosti i poretka u državi od 2 Avgusta 1921" ("Law of the Kingdom of Serbs, Croats, and Slovenes on the Protection of Public Welfare and Order in the State of 2 August 1921"), *Službene novine Kraljavine Srba, Hrvata, i Slovenaca (Official Journal of the Kingdom of Serbs, Croats, and Slovenes)*, III, 170-A (August 3, 1921), 1–2; and Radoljub Čolaković, Dragoslav Janković, and Pero Morača, eds., *Pregled istorije Saveza komunista Jugoslavije (Survey of the History of the League of Communists of Yugoslavia)* (Beograd: Institut za izučavanje radničkog pokreta, 1963), pp. 69–77.

the people."[18] This sentiment was taken to be a personal appeal to King Alexander to assume dictatorial power in order to assure social order. Considering the explosiveness of the situation, a brief attempt was made to pacify the Croats by appointing a compromise Slovene Prime Minister. Despite this maneuver, the major outcome was the assumption of full dictatorial powers by King Alexander. To undermine the strong feeling of ethnic division, a territorial reorganization of the kingdom was instituted. This involved dividing the country into *banovine* that would cut across traditional provincial boundaries; each such *banovina* was to have its own *ban* or governor appointed by the King. The hope of the regime was that this maneuver would help to strengthen the "Yugoslav" dimension of the country. In effect, King Alexander's edicts of 1929 brought to an end what semblance of democracy had existed in Yugoslavia. The *skupština* or assembly was dissolved, political parties were banned, and freedoms of speech and assembly were severely curtailed.[19]

A modicum of constitutional authority was re-established by the promulgation of the 1931 Constitution, which remained in effect until World War II.[20] The *banovine* first instituted in 1929 were retained, and all political movements with ethnic, class, or religious bases were forbidden. Again the purpose was to curb

[18]C. A. Macartney and A. W. Palmer, *Independent Eastern Europe* (London: Macmillan and Co., Ltd., 1962), p. 225.

[19]J. B. Hoptner, *Yugoslavia in Crisis, 1934–41* (New York: Columbia University Press, 1962), pp. 6–8.

[20]"Ustav Kraljevine Jugoslavije od 3 Septembra 1931" ("Constitution of the Kingdom of Yugoslavia of 3 September 1931"), Law no. 427, *Službene novine Kraljevine Jugoslavije (Official Journal of the Kingdom of Yugoslavia)*, XIII, 207–LXVI (September 9, 1931), 1305–14.

"tribalistic" and separatist tendencies and to exalt "Yugoslavia," which had been proclaimed in October, 1929. To buttress the new edifice a government party called the Yugoslav Peasant Radical Democratic Party was formed in 1933; this was later simplified to the more appropriate Yugoslav National Party and served as a facade for control of politics by the Regency. This organization was composed mainly of old coalition elements that had become increasingly atomized; as a result, it tended to become a party dominated by strong personalities but without any effective popular base.

The assassination of King Alexander in 1934 created the opportunity for a rapprochement between the Croat Peasant Party and the Belgrade government. However, instead of pursuing this end, the Stojadinović government chose alliance with the Slovene People's Party, the Moslem Party, and other splinter Serbian groups. The Stojadinović posture succeeded in unifying many Serb and Croat elements into the United Opposition at the head of which stood the Croat Peasant Party, suggesting perhaps that traditional cleavages might be reconciled, given the right conditions and critical issues. In fact, Maček, speaking for the United Opposition in 1938, was hailed in Belgrade by a Serb audience for his stand against police terror. By 1938 the United Opposition was able to mobilize an impressive 1,364,524 votes as against 1,643,783 for the slate of government candidates.[21] Owing in part to the pressures exerted by the United Opposition, but primarily to the growing influence of Nazi Germany, the Regency attempted a settlement of the Serb-Croat dispute by the *sporazum*

[21]Čulinović, *Yugoslavia Between the Two Wars*, II, 131–33; and, for election data by "Banovine," see: *Statistical Yearbook, 1938–1939*, p. 478.

of August, 1939.[22] The purpose of the *sporazum* was to grant wide autonomy to a "new" Croatia, which was to include the Sava and Primorje *banovine* and parts of Bosnia. Although acceptable for the most part to the Croat Peasant Party, the *sporazum* was anathema to nearly all Serb politicians as well as to extreme Croat chauvinists.[23]

The pattern of rule from 1929 on continued to intensify national hatreds and conflict. The Yugoslav Regency, by attempting to stand above the conflict, had succeeded merely in alienating all parties to it. Local prefects ruled by the authority and power of the central government alone; the swollen civil service in conjunction with the army constituted the chains that kept the country from disintegrating. Recognizing that social order could not be achieved by relying upon traditional institutions, and lacking a period of experimentation with democratic forms, the Yugoslav government had little recourse but to resort to instruments of force. The attempt to contrive a "new" foundation for a "new Yugoslavia" in 1931 was a noble one despite its biases and its failure. Of the regional forces only the Slovenes and Dalmatians for whom a unified state seemed to be necessary for survival failed to develop a strong separatist movement. After 1929 the govern-

[22]The text of the "sporazum" ("agreement") is published in Dragiša Cvetković, ed., *Srpsko-Hrvatsko pitanje i putevi sporazuma (The Serbo-Croatian Question and the Paths of Agreement)* (Paris, 1952), pp. 18–26; and, for a treatment of Vladimir Maček's role in resolving the Croatian question and negotiating with the Italian Minister of Foreign Affairs Count Galeazzo Ciano, see: Hugh Gibson, ed., *The Ciano Diaries, 1939–1943; The Complete, Unabridged Diaries of Count Galeazzo Ciano, Italian Minister of Foreign Affairs, 1936–1943* (Garden City: Doubleday and Co., 1946).

[23]Hoptner, *Yugoslavia in Crisis,* pp. 151–55.

ment was opposed even in Serbia proper, with a Serb separatist movement becoming increasingly evident. Perhaps unavoidably the country had to await a second political foundation—one that was uniquely "Yugoslav"—before shared institutions could become operative.

Integration Pattern with Other States

Now we must examine the direction and scope of Yugoslav affiliation and integration with other states. If we look at history, we find that Serbian tactics involved developing close ties with Russia and France in order to counter pressures exerted upon her by Austro-Hungary and Germany. However, another factor was operative that made securing this balance difficult—namely, the reliance of South Slavs upon the Austro-Hungarian and German economies for sale of raw materials and livestock as well as purchase of goods. Generally, the interwar pattern shows a trend away from political ties with Russia and France and toward closer relations with Germany.

The Yugoslav policy immediately after World War I was directed toward creating a power base in the Balkans; therefore the Little Entente was conceived as a bulwark against the pressure of major powers in this region.[24] In addition to combining the efforts of Yugo-

[24]The Little Entente was formed in 1920–21 through a series of bilateral agreements between Czechoslovakia and Yugoslavia (August 4, 1920), Rumania and Czechoslovakia (April 23, 1921), and Yugoslavia and Rumania (June 7, 1921). It became obsolete and ineffective with the signing of the Munich Agreement (September 29–30, 1938) by the great powers. For a good treatment of Balkan unions and full texts of the agreements, see: Theodore I. Geshkoff, *Balkan Union: A Road to Peace in Southern Europe* (New York: Columbia University Press, 1940), Part III

slavia, Czechoslovakia, and Rumania, the Little Entente had the clear support of one of the major powers —namely, France. The immediate goal of the Little Entente was to stabilize Balkan politics against the "revisionist" ambitions of Hungary and Bulgaria. Regional co-operation and the Yugoslav power base were further enhanced by the creation of the Balkan Entente; this new Entente, which was directed largely against Bulgarian designs, included Yugoslavia, Greece, Rumania, and Turkey. In addition to the usual treaty commitments, a permanent council as well as an economic advisory council were established. Later the Balkan Entente also created a marine commission and laid out plans for regional postal, telegraph, and telephone unions.[25] Although conceived largely as measures to counter Italy, Hungary, and Bulgaria, these efforts in regional co-operation involved a serious attempt to co-ordinate specific aspects of common action and policy in the Balkans.

This pattern of interstate association for Yugoslavia continued until the mid-1930's; a new pattern began to emerge by 1935 with Germany as the catalyst. Although British and French funds had been extensively invested

---

on the Ententes, and the Appendices for texts of the agreements. Also see: Andrew Gyorgy, *Governments of Danubian Europe* (New York: Rinehart and Co., 1949), and, Seton-Watson, *The East European Revolution.*

[25]The Balkan Entente was founded by four Balkan powers— Yugoslavia, Rumania, Greece, and Turkey—with signing of the Balkan Pact in Athens on February 9, 1934. With conclusion of the German-Soviet Agreement (August 23, 1939), the Balkan Entente was dealt its first blow, and with Rumania's adherence to the Tripartite Pact (November 23, 1940), its final coup de grâce. For the text of the agreement, see: Geshkoff, *Balkan Union,* pp. 300–10.

in Yugoslavia, neither country could provide Yugoslavia with an adequate outlet for her wealth of raw materials. As a result, increasingly larger amounts of Yugoslav raw materials were being sold to Germany; this of course intensified Yugoslav economic dependence upon the German market and economy. Accordingly, by 1938 we find that Yugoslav imports from Germany constitute 32.5 per cent of her trade, and Yugoslav exports to Germany account for 35.9 per cent of her foreign market.[26] Such extensive economic dependence, coupled with impressive German political and military pressures, presented Yugoslav leaders with more than a few problems (see Table 8). With the Munich sellout and German occupation of the Sudetenland, the Yugoslav regime felt that a policy of accommodation in relation to Germany might be tactically sound. After all, the behavior of France and Britain had given a certain international legitimacy to the role of appeaser.

The rising tensions between Yugoslavia and its neighbors could be explained at least in part as outgrowths of ethnic minority problems. Accordingly, while the Yugoslavs claimed the largely Slavic-speaking populations of Istria and Gorizia, Italy continued to assert its historic right to the ancient Roman province and formerly Venetian territory of Dalmatia. Similarly, Hungary made it known that large sections of the Vojvodina rightfully belonged to her; as a result, both the Croatian Ustaši and Hungarian irredentists in Yugoslavia were openly encouraged as well as surreptitiously assisted.[27] Finally, a Macedonian separatism and

[26]*Statistical Yearbook, 1938–1939*, pp. 252–53.
[27]Macartney and Palmer, *Independent Eastern Europe*, pp. 312–13.

Bulgarophilism, espoused by the revolutionary IMRO and backed by Sofia, contributed to strained relations between Bulgaria and Yugoslavia. Despite these conflicts, the specter of German power and influence coupled with British-style appeasement effectively forced Yugoslavia into a posture of accommodation in relation to these states. The result was that Yugoslavia was to lose the regional basis of power that she had worked to develop over the years.

The catering by Allied Powers to German designs and ambitions dealt a deathblow to the effectiveness of Balkan regional arrangements. Accordingly, we find that the sellout and collapse of Czechoslovakia destroyed the Little Entente as an operative and effective Yugoslav alliance. In similar fashion, the pressure to come to terms with "revisionist" states (namely, Hungary and Bulgaria) increased, which, in turn, effectively undermined Yugoslav commitments to Rūmania, Greece, and Turkey. The process of decay was helped along considerably by the timidity of British and French support of the Little and Balkan Ententes in the face of German threats. The Yugoslav government also found itself willing to meet certain demands made upon it by Italy; this included negotiating a Concordat with the Vatican, which created a nation-wide scandal. The over-all result was not merely to alienate traditional and established allies abroad but also to lose the confidence of the Yugoslav people at home. Having thus destroyed both its regional and its domestic basis of power, the Yugoslav government saw no alternative but to turn to the Axis Powers.

In response to immediate pressure from Germany, and after months of deliberation, the Cvetković government on March 25, 1941, capitulated and signed the

Tripartite Pact.[28] We find, however, that the Yugoslavs (Serbs and Croats alike) were apparently not quite
so impressed with German power as were their leaders.
Mass demonstrations occurred in several cities, mobilizing the sentiment of the people and gaining
much international sympathy for the Yugoslav di-
lemma. With the help of Serb military leaders, they
managed to wrest governmental control from the Cvetković forces and soon after to repudiate the Pact and
the Axis Powers. The boldness and heroism of this
deed was to be surpassed in dramatic intensity only by
the tragedy that followed in its wake.

Interwar Yugoslavia was characterized by growing
isolation of the central power in Belgrade from the
political and social forces of the country. Ethnic tension
and conflict represented the clearest disintegrative and
the most volatile force; this was further reinforced by
the growing opposition of all (including many Serb)
parties to the interwar Yugoslav regime. None of the
important interwar parties had a truly national—that
is, a genuinely Yugoslav—character; furthermore, none
offered a program for modernizing the regime or a
basis for reconstituting the state along democratic
lines. The mass parties (for example, Croat Peasant)
in both Serbia and Croatia were based upon peasant
support, which meant they were traditional in orientation, catering to time-honored myths and prejudices.
Middle-class parties, with a somewhat more contempo-

[28]The text of Yugoslav accession to the Tripartite Pact (signed
at Belvedere in Vienna, Austria, on March 25, 1941), reads:
"Yugoslavia adheres to the Tripartite Pact between Germany,
Italy, and Japan, signed in Berlin 27 September 1940." The
agreement was published in the German documents collection
Der Feldzug auf dem Balkan (Berlin: AOK, 1941), p. 15; see
also: Čulinović, *Yugoslavia Between the Two Wars*, pp. 171–94.

rary approach to politics, were confined to the town and city intelligentsia; however, they also tended to be sharply fragmented along traditional ethnic and political lines. Although both the Communist and Socialist parties promised fundamental changes in Yugoslav society, neither one of them represented an effective or fully articulate movement. The stagnation of the economy, combined with the effect of the world depression, limited the effect of the labor movement in politics even beyond limits set by the repressive measures of the central government.

After World War II the old parties, with the bulk of their leadership residing in London, continued the disputes bequeathed to them from the interwar period. They offered no viable solution to the problem of ethnic hostility, a problem that was intensified by the atrocities and massacres of the war. The Communist Party, on the other hand, was largely a new and revitalized organization; its rapid growth and success during the war meant that many new Party members were attracted by the partisan resistance and its solution to traditional ethnic division. The attempt to blend the interwar political tradition with that of the partisans through a coalition of elements from the London government-in-exile proved unfruitful and lasted only a few months. In November of 1945 the People's Front received more than 90 per cent of the vote in a single list election; disillusioned and finding it difficult to offset communist partisan momentum, the interwar political elements gradually withdrew or were driven out of political life.[29] With the adoption of a constitution

[29]For a Yugoslav assessment of this controversial period see: Franjo Tudjman, *Stvaranje socialističke Jugoslavije (The Creation of Socialist Yugoslavia)* (Zagreb: Naprijed, 1960).

in 1946, a new and revolutionary phase begins in Yugoslav politics. The Federal People's Republic of Yugoslavia represented a sharp departure from the patterns of interwar Yugoslavia and was to become in many ways unique even among the new regimes of Eastern Europe.

3: THE PERIOD OF INTENSIVE SOCIALIST DEVELOPMENT

New Demographic Patterns

The second period—that of intensive socialist development—has been defined as including the years 1945 to 1949. In this period, the concern with rapid progress at home, based upon a more or less purist version of the Marxist socioeconomic model, was accompanied by a "hard line" in international politics. From the demographic standpoint, some of the sensitive problems of interwar Yugoslavia seemed to be solved by the tragedy of World War II. First of all, the large unreliable German ethnic minority had been virtually eliminated, either by expulsion or by self-imposed flight. Secondly, co-ordination of Serb and Croat effort during the war under the common banner of the *partizani* created a new sense of camaraderie; the effect of the latter was to generate a shared myth of political foundation as the basis for new authority.[1]

Despite the loss of over 1,700,000 Yugoslav lives dur-

[1]Two examples of such mythical constructions are Franjo Tudjman, *Stvaranje socijalističke Jugoslavije (The Creation of Socialist Yugoslavia)* (Zagreb: Naprijed, 1960); and Blagota Drašković, *Socijalistička revolucija u Jugoslaviji (The Socialist Revolution in Yugoslavia)* (Zagreb: Znanje, 1960).

ing the war, the population of the country in 1948 stood at 15,772,000, which was about 200,000 greater than indicated by 1939 figures.[2] By 1948 the death rate had been reduced to 13.5 deaths per thousand inhabitants, which compared favorably to the 1939 figure of 14.9 (see Table 4). Furthermore, the birth rate in 1948 was somewhat higher at 28.1 than was the case in Yugoslavia during the late 1930's; for example, 25.9 live births per thousand inhabitants were indicated for 1939.[3] The lower death rate in conjunction with a higher birth rate suggests significant natural growth for a country just recovering from the ravages of war; although in 1939 the natural increase ratio was only 11.0, by 1948 it had risen to 14.6 per thousand inhabitants.[4] Consistent with the postwar need for development, and in light of the Marxist emphases upon industry and the professions, a movement of people away from the villages and toward urban and industrial centers began. The burgeoning of population in certain urban regions, such as Zagreb and Belgrade, gave evidence of this, so that by 1948 the latter could boast of nearly 400,000 inhabitants.

As a result of its participation in the war Yugoslavia had received the territories of Istria and Venezia Giulia with the exception of Trieste and environs. This involved the transfer to Yugoslavia of more than 300,000 persons living in an area of 7,728 square kilometers; however, this territory also brought approximately

[2]Savezni zavod za statistiku (Federal Bureau of Statistics), *Statistički bilten (Statistical Bulletin)*, no. 1 (July, 1950), pp. 16–17.

[3]Savezni zavod za statistiku (Federal Bureau of Statistics), *Statistički godišnjak FNRJ, 1955 (Statistical Yearbook FPRY, 1955)* (Beograd, 1955), p. 67.

[4]*Statistical Yearbook, 1962*, p. 55.

100,000 dissident Italians into Yugoslavia.[5] The compromise French demarcation that had settled the dispute also left about the same number of Slovenes within the frontiers of Italy. Since diplomatic efforts failed to gain agreement on the permanent status of Trieste itself, the "free territory" principle seemed the sensible approach for buying time and avoiding direct confrontation.

As indicated above, Yugoslav minority problems were alleviated somewhat by the events of World War II. The percentage of inhabitants in Yugoslavia classifiable as "national minorities" dropped from 14.8 in 1931 to 12.6 in 1948, which seems a significant reduction.[6] However, Yugoslavia still had the largest percentage of minority elements of any country in Western or Central Europe (see Table 1). The major changes in demography occurred with respect to the German and Turkish minorities in Yugoslavia. From over half a million before the war the German minority was reduced (primarily through expulsion and flight) to about one-tenth that number. Owing primarily to emigration the Turkish population by 1948 was reduced to less than a hundred thousand. Statistics also indicate a sharp reduction in the number of Rumanians living in Yugoslavia after the war, although this seems to be due mainly to the introduction of a new category—namely, the Vlachs—that the 1931 census

[5]The 1948 census indicated that Yugoslavia still had 79,573 Italians within its borders, although by this time many of them had already emigrated to Italy. *Statistical Bulletin,* no. 1 (July, 1950), pp. 16–17.

[6]These percentages are derived from a compilation based upon official Yugoslav statistics in George W. Hoffman and Fred W. Neal, *Yugoslavia and the New Communism* (New York: Twentieth Century Fund, 1962), p. 29.

had not included; according to the 1948 census about 103,000 Latin-speaking Vlachs were to be found in Yugoslavia.[7] The vacuum left by these population withdrawals (primarily, of the Germans from the Vojvodina) opened up new areas for resettlement by Yugoslavs.

The large Albanian minority, already of major concern to the interwar Yugoslav regime, increased in number to more than 750,000, or 4.8 per cent of the total population. The Yugoslav communist state therefore found it expedient to create the autonomous region of Kosovo-Metohija (Kosmet), where the larger part of the Albanian minority lives. The census figures for 1948 indicate that about 65 per cent of the total population in Kosmet listed Albanian as its native language. Located primarily in the Vojvodina, the Magyar-speaking population numbered over 496,000 according to the 1948 census; although increasing in absolute terms, the Magyar minority was about the same proportionately as before the war. If the Vojvodina were considered alone, however, in 1948 the Magyars still made up about one-third of its inhabitants.[8] Other ethnic minorities that counted 50,000 or more included Slovaks, Gypsies, Bulgarians, and Russians.

Among the major Slavic groups in Yugoslavia the Serbs numbered 6,547,000, the Croats 3,784,000, the Slovenes 1,415,000, the Macedonians 810,000, and the Montenegrins 426,000—all based upon 1948 figures.[9]

[7]*Statistical Bulletin,* no. 1 (July, 1950), pp. 16–17.

[8]For an extensive and useful discussion of minorities in Yugoslavia, see: Ljubiša Stojković and Miloš Martić, *National Minorities in Yugoslavia* (Belgrade: Publishing and Editing Enterprise "Yugoslavia," 1952).

[9]*Statistical Bulletin,* no. 1 (July, 1950), pp. 16–17.

A distinct group of about 809,000 persons constituted a "Yugoslavs undeclared" category; mostly, these represented Slavic-speaking Moslems in Bosnia-Hercegovina, who did not wish to be identified either as Serbs or as Croats. Generally, the religious pattern remained much the same as during the interwar period; the Orthodox constituted the largest group, which included Serbs, Montenegrins, Macedonians, Bulgarians, Rumanians, and Russians; the Catholics as the second largest religious group were comprised of Slovenes and Croats; and the Moslems counted among themselves the Albanians, Islamicized Slavs, and Turks.[10] A minor change involved a reduction in the number of Protestants, which can best be explained by the virtual elimination of the German minority in Yugoslavia. Finally, the genocide policy of the nazis and Croatian fascists practically eliminated the already small Yugoslav Jewish population (see Table 3). Surely of major significance is that after the war an increasingly larger number of Yugoslavs of all confessions declared themselves as having no religious affiliation.

Consistent with a desire to project a progressive image, and as a result of an intensified educational program, Yugoslav statistics show a rather astounding reduction in illiteracy figures. Although the 1931 census revealed that 44.6 per cent of the populace was illiterate, by 1948 this figure had declined to 25.4, which represents a rather impressive gain.[11] This increased literacy also corresponded with the continued strong movement of people toward urban and industrial cen-

[10]For a discussion of religious groups in Yugoslavia, see: Rastko Vidić, *The Position of the Church in Yugoslavia* (Beograd: Publicističko izdavački zavod "Jugoslavija," n.d.).

[11]*Statistical Yearbook, 1958,* p. 80.

43

ters. Literacy of course becomes a crucial factor for any system that has hopes for achieving rapid industrial progress. Despite the severe reduction of German and Turkish minorities, the remaining Albanian and Magyar enclaves still confronted the new Yugoslav state with difficult issues to resolve. The Albanians, as well as representing the largest ethnic minority in Yugoslavia, tended also to be the most conservative and the most illiterate. This of course made it difficult to integrate the Albanian element into the social and economic complex of Yugoslavia as an aspiring industrial state.

Revitalized Belief Patterns

The belief system that guided Yugoslav leaders after the war was dominated by two goals: (1) to create a truly unified South Slavic state, and (2) to realize the Soviet vision or model of a socialist system. Having been victims as well as beneficiaries of internal Yugoslav strife, partisan leaders were sensitive to time-honored hostilities between Serbs and Croats. Even a communist Yugoslavia they felt would not be able to survive without some basic unity of tradition and historical experience. Therefore, as well as generating unity by stressing the sharing of past war experience, the partisan leadership also employed the imagery of a shared future vision. It was essential not only to have suffered together in the past, but also to anticipate the moment when the fruits of sacrifice would be realized.

The integrative force primarily instrumental in overcoming traditional ethnic strife was the shared experience of partisan resistance.[12] To become a partisan it

[12]Accordingly, Dedijer, in discussing the foundation of the new state, spends most of his time dramatizing the experience of partisan resistance. In so doing, he contributes significantly to

was not necessary to specify that one was a Serb, Croat, Slovene, Moslem, or whatever; neither was it necessary to declare oneself a communist. On the other hand, a Mihailović Četnik by his very association declared to all that he was a Serb in addition to being for the restoration of the monarchy. Surely, the bonds that develop between comrades under fire confronting a common enemy (namely, the German invader) are not easily dissolved; co-operation in the face of death usually erases feelings of ethnic separatism. Accordingly, out of these tragic wartime experiences developed what might be termed a *partisan myth of solidarity*. Given a reality by the passion and suffering of battle, this myth not only served to bind together the leaders of the communist movement, but also helped to solidify the lower echelon, noncommunist rank and file behind a common "Yugoslav" cause. After the war, this glorification of the heroic struggle against the invader was combined with denunciation of traditional interwar parties and their leaders as separatists, traitors, and collaborators.[13] The partisan experience, therefore, was not

the myth of political founding which stands as the basis of the Yugoslav socialist system. Vladimir Dedijer, *Tito* (New York: Simon and Schuster, 1953). See also: Josip Broz Tito, *Borba za oslobodjenje Jugoslavije, 1941–1945) (Struggle for the Liberation of Yugoslavia, 1941–1945)* (Beograd: Kultura, 1947); and Vladimir Dedijer, *Dnevnik (Diary)* (Beograd: Jugoslovenska knjiga, 1951).

[13]Some authorities have questioned the military contribution made by the partisans to the Allied cause during World War II. David Martin provides statistics indicating that Yugoslav losses during the war were 1,695,000 dead, of which only 283,540 died on the battlefield. In contrast, the highest figure given by Allied sources for Germans killed and missing in the entire Balkan area during the war was 30,000. These observers, however, would tend to overlook the nuisance value and psychological force that any such resistance movement in fact contributes. See: David Martin, *Ally Betrayed—The Uncensored Story of Tito and Mihailovich* (New York: Prentice-Hall, 1946).

simply beneficial and effective as a movement of resistance; it was also invaluable as a political-founding myth that delimited the basis of the new postwar structure of authority. A true Yugoslav state could not have an effective basis until all *jugo-slaveni* somehow shared in the sacrifice that brought it to life.

The shared experience of partisan resistance, however, could not fully or alone eliminate feelings of ethnic separatism. The images of Serb massacring Croat, and Croat exterminating Serb, were still too immediate and vivid to permit such naivete and forgiveness. The old tensions were still there, and the war experience irrevocably verified this fact by the ugly spectacle of fratricide. Harsh repressive measures were thus taken against interwar parties and politicians who might rekindle ethnic hatred; any political movements based primarily upon ethnic or religious affiliation were viewed as corrupting and dangerous. The communist regime gained effective support for this policy among young intellectuals, the peasantry, and, generally, those to whom the horrors of fratricidal war were most real. Furthermore, the communist leaders pointed out that no effective solution to the problem of ethnic separatism had been offered by the interwar parties. A genuine fear of the collapse of all social and political order arising from a renewed intranational massacre encouraged these firm measures and policies. Accordingly, the communist regime felt it imperative to crush major Serb and Croat parties and, by so doing, to solve or at least to attenuate the Serb-Croat conflict.

Another aspect of belief that cemented Yugoslav efforts during this period was the Marxist vision of the future. The regard held by Yugoslav communist leaders for Stalin and the Soviet system was only slightly less than religious adulation and spiritual reverence. The figure of Stalin loomed as a hero-legislator through whose inspiration and guidance a new socialist utopia based upon the Soviet model could be instituted. As a result, the Yugoslav communist state became the model satellite in its commitment to the ideals of Marxist industrial society; all sectors of society and economy were to be pushed as rapidly as possible in order to realize this vision. This emphasis upon industry and development proved attractive to the industrial worker and the civil servant, as well as to the growing number of energetic university students and intellectuals now uprooted from the villages. The rejection by these students of the more traditional forms and values had left a convenient normative vacuum that Marxist ideals could rapidly fill. The concept and feeling that a strong Yugoslavia had to be a modern, industrialized, highly educated country provided a focus for a new patriotism; this progressive view also gave the intelligentsia a new sense of purpose and commitment, as well as an arena in which they might feel secure and needed within the context of a forward-looking Yugoslavia. Ultimately, this new patriotism was to be further strengthened by the nature of the Yugoslav-Cominform split. Not surprisingly, therefore, the Yugoslavs stressed the economic aspect of the dispute, which generated a basis for appeal at home, first, on grounds of a policy against Great Power expansionism and, second, in terms of defending proper conditions for economic progress within Yugoslavia.[14] This broad visionary appeal to industrial progress was counterposed to some degree

[14]For documentation and analysis relating to the Soviet-Yugoslav split, see: Robert Bass and Elizabeth Marbury, eds., *The Soviet-Yugoslav Controversy, 1948–1958: A Documentary Record* (New York: Prospect Books, 1959); and Adam B. Ulam, *Titoism and the Cominform* (Cambridge: Harvard University Press, 1952).

by a passive hostility on the part of the peasantry when it was confronted with the possibility of collectivization. On the whole, however, many elements in the country at least initially seemed to be satisfied with the vision of industrial progress offered by communist leaders.

With respect to the integrative force of Marxist values, two problems remained—one peasant, the other religious. Religion formed a barrier to the acceptance of the Marxist belief system primarily in the Catholic regions of Slovenia and Croatia. Largely because of its international affiliation, in addition to its extensive property holdings, the upper Catholic hierarchy in particular stood militantly opposed to accommodation with the communist regime. On the other hand, the Orthodox clergy did not present itself as a formidable obstacle to communist ambitions, since traditionally it had relied upon the state for its survival. Significantly, there was also widespread participation in the partisan resistance by the lower clergy of both Catholic and Orthodox confessions, which somewhat mollified religious opposition at the lower levels. Finally, the Moslems seemed to be quite accommodating, since they felt that they were much better off under the new regime than they had been under the old. As for the peasantry, it had cultivated a tradition of hostility against *the* central authority for several centuries; therefore, most maneuvers by the state were perceived as deliberate tricks contrived to destroy the "old ways."[15] Consequently, the ideo-

[15]Several authors who examine this problem of peasant resistance to change in Yugoslavia include: Ruth Trouton, *Peasant Renaissance in Yugoslavia, 1900–1950* (London: Routledge and Kegan, 1952); Ranko Brašić, *Land Reform and Ownership in Yugoslavia, 1919–1941* (New York: Mid-European Studies Center, 1954); Mijo Mirković, *Ekonomska historija Jugoslavije (Eco-*

logical impact of the communist regime was relatively insignificant during this early period. The peasant for the most part remained passively hostile but still unified against encroachments into village life by central authority and its agencies. Ideologically, the communists were also willing to let things stand in the village, since a natural erosion of "old ways" was already under way with the flow into urban centers of young people seeking better opportunity. A significant factor introducing caution into communist policies toward the peasant was also that many leaders of the new regime were themselves of peasant origin.

The Communist Party of Yugoslavia began this period with enormous moral capital in its favor. The years of partisan warfare had given it a solid cadre of party members who had won state power by what they considered to be their own effort. From the very beginning partisan literature *de*-emphasized the role of Western military aid as well as the importance of Soviet armed forces, which was at least in part a Yugoslav response to Soviet allegations that the partisan contribution to the war effort was minimal. In the early years, the Yugoslavs stressed the fact that they were the only Communist Party in Europe to have come to power by their own effort and in their own right. The Yugoslav sacrifice during World War II dramatized a political founding that was unique among all socialist countries; the shared legends about heroic battle with the enemy (consistent with the Balkan epic tradition) cemented a basis upon which to construct postwar authority. Not only did the partisans combine the efforts

---

nomic History of Yugoslavia) (Zagreb: Ekonomski pregled, 1958); and Jozo Tomasevich, *Peasants, Politics and Economic Change in Yugoslavia* (Stanford, Calif.: Stanford University Press, 1955).

of what seemed to be irreconcilable ethnic and class elements; they also stood alone against what seemed overwhelming odds and in the face of near-sure annihilation. For these reasons, the Yugoslav communists had a somewhat different attitude toward the West, which by its very boldness at times proved to be embarrassing to the Soviet Union.

Yugoslav Copies—Soviet Originals

From the very outset, Yugoslav communists set out to reproduce faithful copies of Soviet institutional forms as early as possible. Two factors worked toward the achievement of this goal. First, the Yugoslavs did not have to go through what has been called a "coalition phase" of governing the new state.[16] The partisan communist control of the broadly based People's Front allowed immediate and effective domination of Yugoslav politics. In addition, any possible competition from interwar parties was stillborn through their refusal to participate in the 1945 election. Second, the large number of foreign-owned enterprises confiscated by German forces allowed easy nationalizing of Yugoslav industry. The Yugoslav communists, therefore, gained nearly immediate control of both economy and polity, allowing rapid progress toward a Soviet-style system.

Perhaps the primary and most immediate problem that confronted the new regime was that of handling traditional ethnic division. For this purpose a federal system was adopted that included six republics (Bosnia-Hercegovina, Croatia, Macedonia, Montenegro, Serbia,

[16]This "coalition phase" of the communist take-over in East European states is developed by Hugh Seton-Watson, *The East European Revolution* (New York: Frederick A. Praeger, 1962), pp. 167–229.

and Slovenia), in addition to two autonomous regions (the Vojvodina and Kosovo-Metohija).[17] In contrast to the *banovine* system of King Alexander, ethnic and historic claims of resident Yugoslav peoples were to be honored and constitutionally guaranteed. The 1946 Constitution recognized all such ethnic groups as separate and respected nations within a federated republican system. This solution followed the Soviet model not only with precision but also with a touching devotion; however, the system was none the less effective and fitting for Yugoslav needs. On the whole, traditional ethnic enmity was reduced (although not eliminated) by this granting of linguistic, cultural, and political autonomy. This task was of course also buttressed by efficient suppression of interwar parties based upon ethnic and religious affiliation.

To comply with the needs of federalism the Yugoslav system of representation involved a bicameral legislature. The two chambers of the federal People's Assembly included, a Federal Council representing the people at large and based upon one delegate for each 50,000 inhabitants, and also a Council of Nationalities consisting of members selected from each republic and autonomous region. The latter, it was thought, would effectively represent the major ethnic or national groups within Yugoslavia. The primary function of the People's Assembly was to select a Presidium that, in turn, appointed the Council of Ministers; the Presidium was also expected to govern between meetings of the People's Assembly. The ministries were divided into two categories—that is, federal, and federal-repub-

---

[17]"Ustav Federativne Narodne Republike Jugoslavije od 31 Januara 1946" ("Constitution of the Federal Peoples' Republic of Yugoslavia of 31 January 1946"), Law no. 54, *Službeni list FNRJ (Official Gazette FPRY)*, II, 10 (February 1, 1946).

lic. The former dealt mainly with foreign matters and with nation-wide communication and transportation problems, whereas the latter integrated activities of the various republics in matters relating to finance, justice, and economy. Country-wide co-ordination was also achieved by committees appointed by the Council of Ministers, the most important being the Federal Planning Commission. In addition, the OZNA or secret police for "defense of the people" enforced the discipline necessary for proper co-operation in a communist state. Finally, the military establishment as an integrative force should be mentioned, with respect both to its function as an educational arena and to its "national" character permitting contacts and mobility. All these structural elements of course betray a rather vivid and predictable likeness to those of the Soviet Union.

Undoubtedly the strongest force guaranteeing integrated effort was the Communist Party of Yugoslavia. Gaining considerable prestige as leader of the resistance movement, the Party immediately took upon itself the role of the main bulwark of the People's Front. Although in theory a coalition of the Communist and other "antifascist" interwar parties, the People's Front was effectively dominated and manipulated by its communist elements. In fact, the Party adroitly employed the People's Front as an instrument by which to expand its base of popular support, just as it used words like "Partisan" and "National-Liberation" to enlist wide support among the people.[18] As a result, the other

[18]The People's Front rapidly expanded its membership until by 1948 it approached the 7,000,000 figure. Similarly, the Communist Party of Yugoslavia indicated rather astonishing growth —from 140,000 members in 1945 to 530,000 in 1949. Hoffman and Neal, *Yugoslavia and the New Communism*, p. 197.

interwar parties (Serb Democrats, Croat Peasant, and so forth) were able to maintain little or no effective political life or organization of their own. Organizationally, the Party articulated party structures in each republic and region that paralleled its country-wide system. Within the state administrative system the Party maintained unofficial control, even though a communist did not always head a section formally. Finally, the heroic image cast by Tito and his comrades during their epic-making resistance helped the Party to widen its popular support. This extensive prestige won during the resistance of course remained central for setting up the postwar regime.

Another problem confronting the new regime was the economic reconstruction of Yugoslavia. Ironically enough, the economic devastation wrought by war sped up the process of nationalizing Yugoslav industry. The bourgeois power base had been undermined or destroyed by enemy expropriation and occupation during the war. Furthermore, the numerous industries controlled by foreign interests, and already confiscated by the German invader, made it rather convenient for a communist-style takeover and transformation of the economy. As for collaborators and war profiteers, their expropriation met with popular approval and even acclaim. For these many reasons, active resistance to nationalization seemed to be all but nonexistent within Yugoslavia.[19] Basic nationalization promulgated by the law of December, 1946, had placed all nationally significant industry, and all transportation and banking,

[19]On the problem of resistance to nationalization, see: Drago Krndija, *Industrializacija Jugoslavije (The Industrialization of Yugoslavia)* (Sarajevo: Ekonomski institut univerziteta u Sarajevu, 1961).

under state management.[20] By 1948 nearly all industry within Yugoslavia was brought under the direct ownership and control of the state. Consistent with their Soviet-style goals, the Yugoslavs attempted to encourage large sectors of the population to abandon rural life and to take up industrial jobs. The Five Year Plan adopted in 1947 envisioned the ultimate transfer of about one million persons to urban centers for work in industrial enterprises. Generally, the new regime exploited opportunities afforded by war devastation and the need for reconstruction to accelerate the process of nationalizing industry.

The peasants of Yugoslavia confronted the new regime with a traditional problem—namely, how to integrate them into the national economy.[21] The standard Marxist vision as expressed in Soviet experience called for extensive development of both state and collective farms. Despite his major contribution to partisan wartime successes, the South Slav peasant continued to cherish his historic right to small individually owned plots. Moreover, few if any large landholders or "kulaks" existed whose large holdings the communist regime could readily seize. The Basic Law on Agrarian Reform and Colonization (August, 1945) required establishing a land pool from which collective and state farms might be set up.[22] These lands were taken mainly

[20]"Zakon o nacionalizaciji privatnih privrednih preduzeća od 5 Decembra 1946" ("Law on Nationalization of Private Economic Enterprises of 5 December 1946"), Law no. 677, *Službeni list FNRJ (Official Gazette FPRY)*, II, 98 (December 5, 1946), 1245–47.

[21]Hoffman and Neal, *Yugoslavia and the New Communism*, pp. 265–98.

[22]"Zakon o agrarnoj reformi i kolonizaciji od 23 Avgusta 1945" ("Law on Agrarian Reform and Colonization of 23 Au-

from the few large farms that did exist and from holdings left behind by the fleeing German minority in the Vojvodina.[23] This initial refusal by Yugoslav communists to push collectivization meant that the small peasant landholder would not be alienated, although he still retained his traditional suspicion of any decision emanating from centralized authority. Before long, however, indirect pressures were applied to encourage the small peasant to join collective farms. Despite these efforts, by the end of 1948 the private sector still accounted for 93.8 per cent of all arable land, whereas state farms held 3.6 per cent and peasant work co-operatives, 2.6 per cent of the balance. As a result, and stemming from Soviet pressures, the communist regime in July, 1948, launched a new drive for collectivization applying somewhat more severe pressures.[24] The maximum effect of this drive by 1951

---

gust 1945"), Law no. 605, *Službeni list DFJ (Official Gazette DFY)*, I, 64 (August 28, 1945), 621–24; see also: Borislav T. Blagojević, ed., "Nationalization and Expropriation," *Collection of Yugoslav Laws*, III (Beograd: Institute of Comparative Law, 1963).

[23]Statistics indicate that 66.2 per cent of all such confiscated lands were taken from large landholders, German proprietors, and various Church holdings. Former German-owned lands alone accounted for 40.7 per cent of the 1945 land pool. *Statistical Yearbook, 1955,* p. 199.

[24]For the nature of economic and other pressures exerted by the Soviet Bloc, see: Ministry of Foreign Affairs, *White Book on Aggressive Activities by the Governments of USSR, Poland, Czechoslovakia, Hungary, Rumania, Bulgaria and Albania towards Yugoslavia* (Belgrade, 1941); and, for the subsequent forced drive to collectivization launched by the Yugoslav government in 1949, see: "Osnovni zakon o zemljoradničkim zadrugama od 6 Juna 1949" ("Basic Law on Agricultural Cooperatives of 6 June 1949"), Law no. 411, *Službeni list FNRJ (Official Gazette FPRY)*, V, 49 (June 9, 1949), 711–21.

showed about 20 per cent of arable land in peasant work co-operatives and approximately 6 per cent in the state farm sector.[25] The peasants met this challenge of intensified collectivization by deliberate lowering of output, thereby warning that such intimidation might well backfire.

For a country emerging from the ravages of war the problem of self-sufficiency is a delicate one. During this period Yugoslav reliance upon external assistance for recovery (namely, upon UNRRA economic aid) was crucial for its survival. Not long after the war, however, transportation and communication facilities, in addition to a small industrial complex, began to provide a degree of economic self-sufficiency. Despite this, the production of crude iron still indicated a significant drop from prewar levels; items such as electrical energy and coal production were also down, if 1946 were to be compared with prewar figures.[26] Certainly, in light of the devastation of war this reduction in productive capacity is something that would be expected. By 1947, however, the Yugoslav industrial index reached a level slightly higher than that recorded for 1939; with this 1939 index set at 100, the 1947 figure indicated a 120.6 level. And, further, by 1948 the production of goods had attained a level (industrial index = 150.3) significantly higher than that recorded for the interwar period (see Table 6). Such a re-establishment of a measure of self-sufficiency was necessary if the new

[25]United Nations, *Economic Survey of Europe in 1953: Yugoslavia* (Geneva, 1954), pp. 106–22.

[26]Accordingly, we find that crude iron production dropped from 101,000 to 84,000 tons between 1939 and 1946; coal production from 7,032,000 to 6,652,000 tons; and production of electrical energy from 1,173,000 to 1,150,000 kilowatt hours. *Statistical Yearbook, 1962,* pp. 142–44.

Yugoslav state was to survive the approaching Soviet-Yugoslav split. Other factors not to be overlooked in assessing Yugoslav self-sufficiency were of course its military establishment and the firm leadership exerted by the Communist Party.

The 1945–49 period indicates a rather uncritical attempt by Yugoslavs to adapt Soviet institutional forms to somewhat unique conditions. Leaders of the Party perhaps wanted too much to develop a satellite that was a faithful replica of the Soviet Union; yet their very experience as an independent partisan movement seemed to belie this effort. Consequently, they apparently gave inadequate attention in this early period to issues and conditions peculiar to Yugoslavia itself. At one point, even Soviet leaders complained that the Yugoslavs were taking the Marxist socioeconomic model somewhat too seriously. Such a purity of vision would seem to come from an innocence inspired by revolutionary striving insulated from a clear understanding of the opportunism characteristic of Great Power behavior. Soviet leaders felt that the Yugoslavs should relax a bit; they should be less virginal, less doctrinaire. Perhaps the realization of the Marxist utopia too quickly might well have proved embarrassing to the Soviet Union itself. In the next period, we shall find that Yugoslav disaffection with the Soviet Union was accompanied by more adaptability at home.

Bloc-Oriented Integration

Yugoslav posture in relation to other states was also affected by its pride in being the model satellite. As a result, not only were its relations with Western powers unduly strained, but it also pursued as close association as possible with other communist party states. Consistent with interwar Yugoslav policy, the new communist regime also tried through regional pacts to establish a power base in the Balkans. The Yugoslav style of aggressive diplomacy might also be traced to the uncompromising sense of national honor and independence intensified by the partisan resistance. Certainly, this factor seems to have been a crucial one in the development of the Soviet-Yugoslav dispute. For those recently sharing the burden of sacrifice, the Yugoslav would argue, the risks involved in a renewed confrontation are always somehow more bearable.

Until the Cominform break in March, 1948, Yugoslavia was considered and viewed itself as the model satellite. It was ruled by a party that came to power by its own effort and in its own right. What is more, the communist (or partisan) resistance force was treated as an ally by the Great Powers during World War II; thus, it did not suffer the stigma of being a former Axis-aligned country, as did some satellite states. For this reason, even sometime unreasonable or extreme demands by the Yugoslavs were directed by way of recognized and respected diplomatic channels. These included demands for Istria and Trieste from Italy, Carinthia from Austria, an autonomous Macedonia from Greece, and general reparation payments for the war. Most of these demands brought the young and somewhat brash state into direct confrontation and conflict with the West. As a matter of fact, during this period Yugoslavia behaved even more aggressively than was to the taste of the Soviet Union, which apparently made it difficult for the Soviet Union to support many Yugoslav claims. The Yugoslav sense of pride was suggested by Moša Pijade when he stated that "certain

leaders of other parties . . . arrived in their free countries in planes with pipes in their mouths, while for
four years, four times daily they vainly called on the
masses to struggle, via radio, while we won our freedom
with arms in our hands."[27] In addition to the Trieste
problem, tensions between Yugoslavia and the West
increased as the result of the shooting down of two
American planes and the killing of five pilots. Curiously enough, both Great Britain and the Soviet Union
saw Yugoslav machinations in Greece as threats, but of
course for quite different reasons, and this despite out-
ward Soviet approval.[28] In addition, Yugoslav intrigue
in the southern Balkans contributed to the development of the Truman Doctrine as the Western instrument for containing communist expansion. Accordingly, tensions between Yugoslavia and the West ran
high, reaching their peak perhaps in 1948, just prior
to the Soviet-Yugoslav break.

The policy and aspirations of communist Yugoslavia
in the Balkans are of special interest. A South Slav or
Balkan Federation combining the forces of Bulgaria
(and, possibly, Albania) was envisioned by Tito; it was
felt that this would give Yugoslavia effective control of
the Balkans as a power base from which to operate and
withstand the pressures of larger states. Understandably, the Great Powers (including the Soviet Union)
looked askance at the possibility of a Balkan power of
such magnitude. A meeting between Tito and Dimitrov had taken place in Belgrade in July, 1947, to dis-
cuss the problems of federation; a month later a treaty
was published providing for close co-operation and abo-

[27]*Borba,* July 10, 1948.
[28]Svetozar Vukmanović, *How and Why the People's Struggle
of Greece Met With Defeat* (London, 1950), pp. 51–54.

lition of passports as preparatory to a customs union. In addition, a "secret clause" envisioned a common state under the name of Union of South Slav Peoples' Republics.[29] Editorially, the Soviet Union responded by asserting that "those countries do not need an artificial and problematic union, federation or customs union."[30] Here, then, the sometimes subtle but always definite pressures from both East and West, coupled with the untimely death of Dimitrov, effectively worked to check Tito's ambitions for developing a power base in the Balkans.

Being the devoted satellite that it was, Yugoslavia tried to cultivate extensive trade with other communist party states. As a result, by 1947 the Soviet Union and its satellites provided Yugoslavia with 51.8 per cent of its imported goods and, in turn, received 49.1 per cent of Yugoslav exports (see Table 8). Significantly, the bulk of imported goods consisted of manufactured items, whereas Yugoslav exports were primarily raw materials and resources useful in manufacture elsewhere. As early as the third quarter of 1949 this pattern had changed radically; imports from communist party states dropped to 3.2 per cent and exports to 7.7 per cent of total Yugoslav foreign trade.[31] This suggests

[29]This was made public in a speech by Tito to the People's Assembly on April 27, 1950. See: *Govor Maršala Tita u Narodnoj Skupštini (Speech of Marshal Tito in the People's Assembly)* (Beograd: Rad, 1950).

[30]*Pravda,* January 28, 1948.

[31]These statistical data are taken from a speech by Tito reported in *Borba,* April 28, 1950. For a more detailed breakdown of trade with the Bloc countries for this period, see: Savezni zavod za statistiku (Federal Bureau of Statistics), *Statistika spoljne trgovine Jugoslavije za 1946, 1947 i 1948 godinu (Statistics on the Foreign Trade of Yugoslavia for 1946, 1947, and 1948)* (Beograd, 1953), pp. xiv, xv.

of course heavy dependence by Yugoslavia upon trade with other communist states just prior to the Soviet-Yugoslav split. These import-export data are all the more illuminating if compared against those for Yugoslav trade prior to the war. Import data for 1938 show that 66.0 per cent of Yugoslav trade was with the combined markets of Austria, England, Italy, Germany, France, and the United States; Yugoslav exports to these same countries in 1938 accounted for 64.9 per cent of its trade.[32] However, the import-export figures for 1948 show that total Yugoslav trade with Western Europe amounted only to approximately 42 per cent of its activity. Although an appreciable drop if compared against prewar figures, this percentage was still higher than that for most other communist party states.[33] Other indices of affiliation and integration (for example, telegram and letter flow) also show a decrease in Western orientation if compared to prewar data.[34] Given the Soviet-Yugoslav dispute and the economic boycott by Soviet Bloc states, the trade and integration pattern of Yugoslavia immediately began to shift toward the West.

Because of the significance of the Soviet-Yugoslav dispute, we must say a word about some of its ramifica-

[32]Kraljevina Jugoslavija (Kingdom of Yugoslavia), *Statistički godišnjak, 1938–1939 (Statistical Yearbook, 1938–1939)* (Beograd: Državna štamparija, 1939), IX, 253–58.

[33]See the data compiled by Hoffman and Neal, *Yugoslavia and the New Communism*, p. 343.

[34]For example, telegram flow to East European Communist Bloc countries from Yugoslavia for 1939 indicated 69,439 units and for 1946 a like number at 69,349 units; on the other hand, Yugoslav telegram flow to the rest of Europe shows a drop from 235,554 to 53,357 units between these same years. Savezni zavod za statistiku (Federal Bureau of Statistics), *Statistički bilten (Statistical Bulletin)*, no. 31 (June, 1954), p. 63.

tions. The Cominform expulsion of the Yugoslav Party (announced on June 28, 1948) apparently took most party members, particularly on lower levels, by surprise. Since March, 1948, serious correspondence and debate had been going on between leaders of the Soviet Union and those of Yugoslavia.[35] Formal accusations against the Yugoslavs involved three major points: that they were pursuing unfriendly policies toward the Soviet Union, that they were not pushing collectivization of agriculture hard enough, and that the Party played a rather poor second fiddle to the People's Front. The Soviets also complained that "Yugoslav security organs have controlled and supervised Soviet representatives in Yugoslavia."[36] However, the Yugoslav view of the dispute stressed rather different aspects. They argued that the more economically advanced members of the Bloc were exploiting the somewhat less developed ones such as Yugoslavia.[37] For the Yugoslavs the various attempts by the Soviet Union to put off Yugoslav industrial development gave unquestionable proof of exploitative attitudes by Soviet leadership. Furthermore, the Yugoslavs also sensed that Soviet leaders were suspicious of and annoyed by their diplomatic successes in the Balkans. Both a projected Yugoslav-dominated Balkan Federation and Yugoslavia's militancy in support of the Greek communist

[35]For documents relating to the Soviet-Yugoslav dispute, see: *Pisma CK KPJ i Pisma CK SKP(b) (Correspondence of CC CPY and Correspondence of CC SCP(b))* (Beograd: Borba, 1948); and The Royal Institute of International Affairs, *The Soviet-Yugoslav Dispute* (London and New York: Oxford University Press, 1948).

[36]See the letter of the Central Committee of the Soviet Party to the Yugoslavs in *Correspondence of CC CPY and Correspondence of CC SCP (b)*, p. 37.

[37]*Borba,* October 12, 1948.

effort were evidence of the overextended ambition of Yugoslav communists. Finally, the Soviet Union was somewhat embarrassed by Yugoslav persistence on the Trieste issue; on the other side of the issue, the Yugoslavs were disappointed at the apparently lukewarm support for their claims by the Soviet Union. Until the final break with the Cominform, the Yugoslavs were repeatedly and naïvely surprised at what seemed to be the unprincipled and "un-Marxian" behavior of a brother communist state.

The integrative pattern for Yugoslavia during the period 1945–49 required turning a loyal face toward the East. At the same time, it called for turning one's back upon the West, which had comprised the historic market for South Slavic trade and the source of much of its culture. The Yugoslavs made no pretense about being cordial to Western capitalist states; they intended to push the communist victory as hard as they could. Mutually beneficial co-operation would be limited for the most part to the newly created "socialist camp"; furthermore, the communist movement had taken on an international aspect and strength only dreamed of by former generations. But few communist leaders realized that any such "international aspect" would ultimately generate its conflict-provoking as well as its integrative forces. The Yugoslavs were quick to learn that differences could arise even between themselves and other comradely states. They also realized that any such differences required an adroit playing of the diplomatic game in Western style.

During this period the intellectuals and the young tended increasingly to reject identification with interwar Yugoslav parties and movements. However, an intense and particularistic nationalism still continued to threaten the basis of the new government.[38] Significantly, no alternative center of authority existed or was thought to exist other than that deriving from the partisans; other elements were either routed during the war or were living much too comfortably in London to generate any following. Even the peasantry, which had never shown a deep trust for or a strong reliance upon the rulers of interwar Yugoslavia, seemed to accept partisan leadership. The Serbian peasants in particular felt a sense of betrayal with respect to the behavior of the Serbian Monarchy, especially as it concerned Prince Paul's collaboration with the Axis powers.[39] Given some vestiges of prewar identification, the role of the Tito-Šubašić transitional regime was useful in providing historical continuity and legitimacy. The real authority of the new regime none the less resided with the prestige of partisan victory and the efficiency of Party organization.

The effect of Yugoslav disaffection with the Cominform was to generate a search for an independent Yugoslav road to socialism. For the 1945–49 period the Yugoslav system had not been appreciably different from those of other East European satellites. However, although for most East European satellite states this period represented a time for political consolidation, the Yugoslavs achieved this with considerable effect during the partisan resistance. The Yugoslav regime could thus move directly toward a Soviet-style scheme, whereas other communist states needed time for political consolidation. Indeed, it would appear that this very desire and capability for rapid progress toward the

[38]Mika Tripalo, "The 'Crisis' of the Young Generation," *Socialist Thought and Practice,* no. 2 (1961), pp. 89–103.
[39]See especially Chap. 21 in Martin, *Ally Betrayed.*

Soviet model of socialism did much to contribute to Soviet-Yugoslav tension. Not long after the split many nonparty intellectuals began to re-enter Yugoslav public life with the signs of relaxation becoming increasingly apparent. Accordingly, the next period—that of the thaw—might be effectively described in terms of a thickening of the social base of a transformed Yugoslav system. The acceptance of the communist regime tended in short to become more generalized among the populace. As a result, many interwar intellectuals (including former critics) and party leaders began to talk about making specific changes rather than totally rejecting the system as it stood.

4: SOVIET-YUGOSLAV DISAFFECTION AND THE RESULTING THAW

Environmental Stabilization

One clear benefit accruing from the Soviet-Yugoslav split was a reassessment by the Yugoslavs of their own system. In so doing, the Yugoslavs discovered they could provide solutions for their own special type of problems. The patriarchs of Moscow would no longer have to haunt the Yugoslavs with a specter of infallibility. As Soviet troops had conducted themselves in Yugoslavia with something less than urbane gentility, treating the populace as well as the partisans with considerable arrogance, so Soviet leaders might well be guilty of ruthlessly exploiting their comrades. Accordingly, new institutional forms as well as an overhauled ideology were contrived to meet these Yugoslav needs. The Yugoslavs of course justified their aberrations and reinterpretations as even more true to Marxism than dogma emanating from the Moscow patriarchate; but they were nonetheless genuine innovations that illuminated the issue of "national communism." Such diversified and bold thinking also broadened the potential field of experience for all satellite states. Accordingly, the West presented itself as a new, unexplored universe waiting to be mined for the wealth of associations it offered.

For analytic purposes the years 1950–56 comprise the period of "thaw" or relaxation of pressures. Many trends that will be discussed had of course already made themselves felt by 1949 or perhaps even earlier. Based upon the 1953 census, the Yugoslav population stood at 16,937,000, an increase of more than 1,000,000 since 1948. The greatest population gains were found among the Serbs (7,066,000), with an increase of better than 500,000. In percentages of total population, the "Yugoslavs undeclared" category also indicated strong advances—namely, to about 1,000,000 or 6 per cent of the Yugoslav people. This may well suggest an increasing tendency at this time to identify oneself as a "Yugoslav" rather than by a narrower ethnicity. Although certainly true in part, this statistic can be explained largely by the fact that most Slavic-speaking Moslems refused to identify themselves either as Serbs or as Croats. Other figures on the various major national groups include Croats, with 3,976,000; Slovenes, with 1,487,000; Macedonians, with 893,000; and Montenegrins, with 466,000.[1] All these major groups indicate population increase over figures compiled for the 1948 census (see Table 1).

The ethnic homogeneity of a given region might be expressed as a percentage of the *predominant* ethnic group in relation to total population (see Table 2). Based upon this criterion, Slovenia among all republics was the most homogeneous with 96.5 per cent of its population being Slovene; on the other hand,

[1]Savezni zavod za statistiku (Federal Bureau of Statistics), *Demografska statistika, 1959 (Demographic Statistics, 1959)* (Beograd, 1962), p. 25.

Bosnia-Hercegovina (as might be expected) was least homogeneous with 44.4 per cent of its population Serbs and 31.3 per cent "Yugoslavs undeclared" most of whom were *muslimani* or Moslems.[2] Understandably, it would be anticipated that the more homogeneous the population, the less likely the occurrence of ethnic strife; thus, as we have seen, inadequate ethnic homogeneity defines a historic problem that continues to plague Yugoslavia. As for the two major non-Slavic groups—namely, the Albanian and the Magyar—between 1948 and 1953 these groups showed only slight population increases.

With respect to religious affiliation, the 1953 census indicates that 2,128,000 Yugoslavs listed themselves as "nonbelievers." Among the various faiths we find, on the other hand, that the Orthodox numbered 6,985,000; the Roman Catholic, 5,371,000; and the Moslems, 2,090,000.[3] Most significant, and perhaps not unexpected, are the relatively larger numbers of so-called nonbelievers, who by 1953 constituted about 12.5 per cent of the Yugoslav populace (see Table 3). For the most part these nonbelievers surely represented Communist Party members, individuals who held politically sensitive jobs, or professional and military personnel. Significantly, the number of both Orthodox and Roman Catholic "believers" indicate a percentage decline if compared against figures for the interwar period. This would of course be explained by the indicated sharp rise in the number of nonbelievers within

[2]*Ibid.*, p. 26.
[3]Savezni zavod za statistiku (Federal Bureau of Statistics), *Popis stanovništva vitalna i etnička obeležja, 1953 (Population Census of Vital and Ethnic Characteristics, 1953)* (Beograd, 1953), I, 278–87.

the Yugoslav communist state resulting from an official policy that discourages religious practice.

Yugoslavia had been exerting *de facto* control over Zone B (that is, the rural area just south of Trieste) since the end of World War II. However, the *de jure* incorporation of this zone into Yugoslavia did not occur until a joint memorandum was issued by the United States, Great Britain, Italy, and Yugoslavia in October, 1954. The demographic effect was formally to bring 62,000 new people into Yugoslavia, mostly Slovene and Croat peasants; it also enlarged Yugoslav territory by 524 square kilometers to its presently constituted boundaries.[4] This solution normalized previously strained relations with the West, allowing Yugoslavia thereby to expand its trade and other relations with Western countries. One should add finally that the population of this region (namely, the Koper and Buje communes) had by 1954 already been effectively integrated into the Yugoslav system.

Natural population increase for Yugoslavia in 1953 stood at 16.0 per thousand inhabitants, which compares favorably with 14.6 indicated by the 1948 census (see Table 4). Contributing to this natural growth were a reduction in death rate from 13.5 to 12.4 and an increase in birth rate from 28.1 to 28.4 in the country as a whole. This Yugoslav population growth would therefore be attributed to natural increase rather than to acquisition of new territory or the influx of new ele-

[4]So-called Zone B was divided by the Yugoslav communist regime between the republics of Slovenia and Croatia. The former obtained 234 square kilometers, 39,000 inhabitants, and a "window" on the Adriatic; the latter gained 290 square kilometers and 23,000 persons. Savezni zavod za statistiku (Federal Bureau of Statistics), *Statistički godišnjak FNRJ, 1955 (Statistical Yearbook FPRY, 1955)* (Beograd, 1955), pp. 385, 387.

ments. Despite attempts to improve the standard of living and health conditions, excessive death rates continued in Kosovo-Metohija (20.5) during this period; death rates above the national average were also found in Macedonia (14.7) and Bosnia-Hercegovina (14.4). On the other hand, the death rate in cities (8.6) was considerably lower when compared with the countryside as a whole (13.0). It is also clear that in the less developed regions of Yugoslavia the high death rates were counteracted by even higher birth rates. We find, therefore, that in backward Kosovo-Metohija a birth rate of 42.5 was recorded as compared with 22.3 in more advanced Slovenia.[5] Consequently, despite high death rates, areas such as Kosovo-Metohija, Macedonia, and Bosnia-Hercegovina still show the highest natural growth of population within the country.

Persistent and accelerated movement from village to urban centers also continued during this period (see Table 5). Based upon 1953 figures, the number of persons involved in agricultural pursuits declined to 10,105,587 or about 60 per cent of the total population.[6] In contrast, the 1948 census had listed 10,793,000 in the agricultural sector, which accounted for 68 per cent of the inhabitants in the country.[7] Furthermore, the percentage of total social product attributable to agriculture between 1947 and 1953 declined by 3.0

[5]*Ibid.*, pp. 67–72.
[6]*Statistical Yearbook, 1964*, p. 85. For a discussion of the implications of population movement for industrial development, see: Drago Krndija, *Industrializacija Jugoslavije (The Industrialization of Yugoslavia)* (Sarajevo: Ekonomski institut univerziteta u Sarajevu, 1961), pp. 235–50.
[7]Savezni zavod za statistiku i evidenciju (Federal Bureau of Statistics and Evidence), *Konačni rezultati popisa stanovništva od 15 Marta 1948 godine (Final Results of the Population Census of 15 March 1948)* (Beograd, 1954), III, xxx.

points from 39.1 to 36.1; this compares with an increase in social product for industry from 33.3 to 35.8 or 2.5 percentage points between these same years.[8] Similarly, the percentage of total social product accounted for by transport, crafts, and trades increased during this period. Coupled with this economic development was the growth of major cities in Yugoslavia, such that by 1953 Belgrade had 469,988 inhabitants and Zagreb, 350,542;[9] this showed an increase for each city of about 100,000 since the 1948 census. With the emphasis upon communes and decentralized economy, a strong movement of population was also indicated toward major towns within the numerous regional communes.

The demographic environment of Yugoslavia was not significantly altered during this period. The ethnic balance newly attained after World War II was stabilized, with the institutional setting giving it a formal expression. The primary increase of population was registered among the Serbs; a somewhat larger number of "undeclared" people was also indicated by the census. The Albanian and Magyar peoples continued to constitute the major non-Slavic ethnic groups—both being well over the 500,000 figure. Most elements of these two ethnic groups were to be found within the two autonomous regions; each group thereby obtained a degree of cultural as well as linguistic self-expression. The religious situation changed little except that a larger sector of Yugoslav society declared itself as "non-

[8]*Statistical Yearbook, 1962,* p. 93. For discussion of the impact of changing demographic structure upon the Yugoslav economy, see: Miloš Macura, "Stanovništvo kao faktor privrednog razvoja" ("Population as a Factor of Economic Development"), *Ekonomska politika FNRJ (Economic Policy FPRY)* (Beograd: Rad, 1957), pp. 86–118.

[9]*Statistical Yearbook, 1955,* p. 374.

believers." Finally, both the accelerated rate of natural population growth and the strong movement of people from the villages to urban areas continued.

Marxist Beliefs Reassessed

Having been set adrift upon an uncertain ideological sea by the split, the Yugoslav communists were forced to reassess their Marxist values. Simply to ape the Soviet model was no longer sufficient, nor did it seem to them to be tolerable. The response was to proclaim the Yugoslav position as orthodox, while condemning the Soviet system as in some sense heretical. This of course provided the Yugoslavs with a certain ideological security in what was then an almost completely hostile world. The new Yugoslav road to socialism, it was felt, could not be constructed by the arbitrary genius of a Marxist prophet, whether he be Yugoslav or Russian. On the contrary, it had to emerge from the tedious application of a new institutional form—namely, decentralized worker control—that seemed more appropriate to Yugoslav conditions. The era of unquestioned, inflexible application of Soviet dogma came to an end with a vigorous attempt at social experimentation.

Conflict and debate usually generate new ideological bases to justify the position taken. This was what happened to the Yugoslavs; finding themselves alone and in battle, they discovered that a rationale was necessary for what some considered to be their heresy. As before, myths surrounding the partisan experience served well under these trying circumstances. To brave storms emanating from Moscow one could easily be reminded of and find solace in common sacrifices made in resisting the German invader. If need be, the Yugoslav people could withstand another assault for the pleasures of national integrity and freedom. Invocation of images dramatizing shared war experience and suffering once again was to unify the Yugoslavs during a crisis. Consequently, after the Soviet-Yugoslav split the communist regime regained the support of many previously disenchanted, noncommunist forces. The uniquely Yugoslav road to socialism, as a freshly contrived vision, was useful in bringing these diverse elements together again. What is more, the Marxist statement on differing material conditions, coupled with the doctrine of socialism in one country, could be used to justify an independent road. It was argued that since material conditions in Yugoslavia were peculiar to it, institutional forms and strategy must also be different from those for other states.

The Yugoslav critique of the Soviet system focused mainly upon overcentralization and state bureaucracy. Instead of reducing the apparatus of a centralized state —that is, working toward its withering away—the Soviet system became increasingly intricate and cumbersome.[10] Because of its bureaucracy and the need for state profits, the Soviet system was represented as a form of "state capitalism" compelled to exploit in order to survive. Soviet leaders had permitted a contradiction to arise within their very socialist midst—namely, that between state bureaucracy and the people themselves. For the Soviet Union other socialist states had to serve, firstly, as sources of raw materials and, secondly, as markets for its manufactured goods. All surplus value must

[10]See Edvard Kardelj, "O narodnoj demokratiji u Jugoslaviji" ("On People's Democracy in Yugoslavia"), *Komunist* (1949), no. 4, pp. 1–83; and, the statements by Boris Kidrić in *Borba,* February 8, 1950.

accrue to the Soviet Union; satellite states in effect must become proletarian states exploited by a "state capitalist" Soviet Union. Therefore, a contradiction or conflict basis developed between the Soviet Union and its own satellites, largely owing to its need for economic exploitation. This became clear to the Yugoslavs when no attempt was made to contribute to their industrial development. The sensible alternative, therefore, was to seek the way independently, since it was felt that many roads to socialism in fact existed.

The Yugoslavs in 1950 began what they felt was a *de*bureaucratizing process. In the form of the workers' councils and communes, social ownership of the means of production was to belong to the people, giving the citizens thereby a larger role in decisions affecting economic development.[11] Self-administration of society would develop as experience was gained through worker participation in economic management. The economic goal called for returning some portion of the surplus value to the producers; it also meant that the enterprise could make decisions relating to allocation of its own resources. Psychologically, the "alienation" created by an impersonal state bureaucracy was to be overcome; since producers would now share directly in management control, they could more easily identify with the product of their labor. It was felt that the state would begin to wither away as the decentralizing proc-

[11]See: Josip Broz Tito, *Workers Manage Factories in Yugoslavia* (Beograd: Jugoslovenska knjiga, 1950). For a comparison of the theoretical basis of the more centralized people's democracies of Eastern Europe in contrast to Yugoslav innovations, see: M. H. Fabre, "L'Unité du Pouvoir d'État en Yougoslavie et dans les Démocraties populaires," *Le régime et les institutions de la république populaire fédérative de Yougoslavie* (Bruxelles: Université Libre de Bruxelles, 1959), pp. 91–101.

ess continued and intensified. The first concrete step in this "withering away" process called for putting management directly in the hands of producers.[12] Furthermore, it was predicted that the Communist Party itself would become increasingly expendable as communes learned how to handle their own affairs. The ultimate result envisioned was a spontaneous growth of social norms and rules governing the local commune, which were merely to be supplemented by laws emanating from central authority. In one sense, the peasants' historic distrust of centralized power returns in different guise with local self-administration of society.

Despite revitalized and widely shared beliefs, old divisive forces were not completely silenced. Regional ethnic chauvinism tended to slide into the background largely as a result of vigorous application of law coupled with an insistence upon an ethnically blind socialist morality. Animosities once typifying Serb-Croat relations were reduced in intensity although they were still present; similarly, religious practices and taboos lost much of their force and justification. In fact, marriages between persons with Moslem and Christian backgrounds, as well as between Catholic and Orthodox, became increasingly common. As well as depriving church organizations of their power through expropriation, the communist regime adopted rather stringent controls against expression of religious big-

[12]Editorial, "Neka pitanja naše teorije o socijalističkoj državi i pravi" ("Some Questions about Our Theory of Socialist State and Law"), *Arhiv za pravne i društvene nauke (Archive for Legal and Social Science)* (1950), no. 3, p. 396. For exposition of basic principles underlying Yugoslav "socialist democracy," see: Edvard Kardelj, *Socialistička demokratija u Jugoslovenskoj praksi (Socialist Democracy in Yugoslav Practice)* (Beograd: Kultura, 1954).

otry. Openly manifested religious antagonisms and ethnic conflicts therefore became a crime and were punishable by law. With the slow demise of religious identity the communist regime hoped that religion-based conflict would soon disappear altogether.

Changing patterns of interaction due to economic activity must unavoidably affect more basic levels of society. As a result, value conflicts in villages have become a major factor of daily life in Yugoslavia and a basic problem in its development. This problem has been manifested in a multitude of forms: traditional versus modern, church versus regime, peasant farmers versus collective farmers, and patriarchs versus the young.[13] Attempts have of course been made to reconcile these dichotomies and value conflicts; ultimately, however, the solution has to lie with developing an industrialized society and a modern urban culture. When a system undergoes rapid industrial change, such value conflicts usually occur with considerable frequency and intensity. However, despite these points of tension, certain other factors in Yugoslavia attenuated the severity of divisions and value conflicts. Nurtured by historical tradition and epic poetry, the Yugoslav ethos had demanded that at times one choose "the heavenly kingdom" with the good King Lazar.[14] And,

[13]For analysis of some of these value conflicts and contradictions, see: Bogdan Vidaković, "Neki problemi u razvoju proizvodne saradnje izmedju poljeprivrednih organizacija i individualnih proizvodjača" ("Some Problems in the Development of Productive Cooperation between Agricultural Organizations and Individual Producers"), *Socijalizam* (1963), nos. 5–6, pp. 74–98.

[14]For collections of relevant epic literature, see: Vuk Stefanović Karadžić, *Srpske narodne pesme (Serbian Folk Tales),* 4 vols. (Beograd: Prosveta, 1953–58); and George Rapall Noyes, *Heroic Ballads of Serbia,* trans. G. R. Noyes and Leonard Bacon (Boston: Sherman French and Company, 1913).

as we have seen, a willingness to sacrifice for national honor and integrity was further reinforced by the partisan wartime resistance. Not only did the resistance buttress these old heroic myths, but it also generated a more profound and broader base for co-operation. Furthermore, the brash Yugoslav rebuttal to Stalinist domination also reawakened tradition and generated a new basis for unity. Despite unavoidable value conflicts endemic to any system in transition, certain countervailing forces with roots in historical experience persisted.

Not surprisingly, the Soviet-Yugoslav dispute intensified the Yugoslav tradition and consolidated the country's unity. What emerged as "national communism" (that is, the independent road to socialism) was buttressed by a Yugoslav faith in its partisan resistance. Here the Yugoslav might project affinities with the Serbian revolutionary experience of the nineteenth century or even with the earlier abortive Croat peasant uprising of Matija Gubec. Furthermore, traditional peasant independence may well have its echo in the Yugoslav drive for decentralization. Emphasis upon local self-administration also conforms to the ethnic mosaic of Yugoslavia as well as to its tradition of localism. Finally, the pragmatism of the Yugoslavs was consistent with their weak philosophical tradition; they felt satisfied merely to seek their own way. For the Yugoslavs the uncertainty of social experimentation was more palatable than the tyranny of a fixed model.

Revised Sociopolitical Forms

The guiding purpose of Yugoslav institutional reform was to generate administrative capability at lower levels. By so doing, it was felt that some of the burden of responsibility would be taken off the state machinery; the bureaucratic apparatus would be reduced, and the state could begin to wither away. Accordingly, most Yugoslav institutional innovations were related in some way to the problem of worker participation in local management—the workers' councils, the commune system, and the Council of Producers. We also find a tendency for Party discipline to relax a bit, in addition to a general liberalizing of the political environment. Surely central to the new system was a partial abandoning of representation based upon ethnicity in favor of one more related to economic production. What emerged was a sort of competitive economic pluralism within a matrix of Marxist ideological homogeneity.

The basic institution developed for socialist democracy in Yugoslavia was the workers' council; it was created by a basic law promulgated in July, 1950.[15] The workers' councils varied in size from 15 to 200 members, depending upon the enterprise; election to the councils was by universal suffrage (that is, all members of the enterprise) and by secret ballot. In the smaller enterprises the total work force would constitute the workers' council. Once assembled, the workers' council would select a managing board or directorate from among its own membership. By law three-fourths of the members on managing boards would have to be engaged actively in production; in addition, only one-

[15]"Osnovni zakon o upravljanju državnim privrednim preduzećima i višim privrednim udruženjima od strane radnih kolektiva od 2 Jula 1950" ("Basic Law on the Administration of State Economic Enterprises and Higher Economic Associations from the Standpoint of Workers Collectives of 2 July 1950"), Law no. 391, *Službeni list FNRJ (Official Gazette FPRY)*, VI, 43 (July 5, 1950), 789–93. For an analysis of the workers' council system in Yugoslavia, see: Benjamin Ward, "Workers' Management in Yugoslavia," *The Journal of Political Economy*, LXV (October, 1957), 373–86.

third of its membership could be eligible for re-election. The workers' council in conjunction with trade unions and economic associations also hired the enterprise director (in most cases an "outsider"), whose authority along with that of his staff remained fairly autonomous. As well as being responsible to the enterprise council, the manager would also be held accountable for his work to the commune people's committee. Composition of workers' councils provided for nonparty elements, although major activists were usually members of the Communist Party or of trade unions. Nevertheless, these workers' councils in fact wielded considerable power, especially in matters relating to distribution of premiums and determining enterprise expenditures.[16]

The workers' council system was important to the Yugoslavs for two primary reasons. First of all, it formed one of the better ideological weapons of the communist regime; the Yugoslavs usually stressed workers' councils more than communes as their special contribution to the new road to socialism. Secondly, it involved the more articulate workers in managerial problems, generating a "responsible" attitude towards production.[17] Accordingly, the workers' council af-

---

[16]Branko Horvat and Vlado Rascović, "Workers' Management in Yugoslavia: A Comment," *The Journal of Political Economy,* LXVII (April, 1959), 194–98. For a discussion of problems dealing with workers' control of the factory, see: Georges Friedman, "Problèmes de la Participation ouvrière a la Gestion des Entreprises" and Djordje Mijić, "La Gestion d'Entreprises, Partie intégrante de la Gestion sociale," *Le régime . . . Yougoslavie,* pp. 59–80.

[17]Ivan Božičević, "Necessity and Superfluity of Strikes as a Method and Means of Trade Union Activities under our Constitution," *Socijalizam* (1959), no. 1, *Supplement to Joint Translation Service Bulletin,* no. 2702, March 6, 1959.

forded an opportunity for management experience for the worker, in addition to providing a convenient arena for political education.

Given the decentralizing impact of workers' councils, it became necessary to develop certain *re*centralizing mechanisms. The Party and governmental controls were of course the more obvious and the more available tools for such a task. More subtle and pervasive integrative forces, however, were also provided by the trade unions and by economic associations. Each industry was charged with choosing both regional and industry-wide workers' councils; each of these would then select an administrative committee for the given economic or industrial association.[18] At the top levels, as would be expected, the number of Party members active on these administrative committees tended to increase. In addition, these administrative committees were charged with partial responsibility in hiring directors for individual enterprises, as well as with hearing and judging complaints about the performance of directors. The trade unions also shared in this task of appointing and judging enterprise directors—although somewhat less directly than the associations. Both the economic associations and trade unions tended to have their top-level bodies dominated by Party members, which in effect created an interlocking directorate between the Party and non-Party organizations. The result was to provide the degree of co-ordination necessary to counter any ill effects that might stem from economic decentralization.

[18]Robert Lee Wolff, *The Balkans in Our Time* (Cambridge: Harvard University Press, 1956), p. 393. For the function of trade unions in Yugoslavia, see: Acher Deleon, "La Position et le Rôle des Syndicates de Yougoslavie," *Le régime . . . Yougoslavie,* pp. 166–74.

Basic modifications in the Yugoslav governmental system were achieved by the 1953 Fundamental Law.[19] Federal representation was still effected through the Peoples' Assembly, which contained two chambers— the Federal Council and the Council of Producers. The Federal Council, however, incorporated within itself the old Council of Nationalities, the effect of which was to de-emphasize ethnic representation. The vast majority of delegates to the Federal Council were chosen on the basis of one deputy per 60,000 inhabitants as representatives of the people in general; this was supplemented by delegates selected by the executive bodies of republics and autonomous regions as representatives of national groups.[20] The Council of Producers was drawn from two general economic groupings—the peasants and the workers. Since members of the Council of Producers were selected in terms of contribution to social product, representation was effectively biased in favor of workers and at the expense of the peasantry. These two chambers sitting in joint session chose the Federal Executive committee, which had displaced the old Soviet-style presidium. Hoping to minimize the "new class" effects of bureaucracy, the

[19]*New Fundamental Law of Yugoslavia* (Beograd: Union of Jurists of Yugoslavia, 1953); for an integrated version of the Yugoslav constitution as of 1957, see: *The Constitution of the Federal People's Republic of Yugoslavia* (Beograd: Union of Jurists' Association of Yugoslavia, 1960); and, in Serbo-Croatian, see: *Ustav Federativne Narodne Republike Jugoslavije (Constitution of the Federal People's Republic of Yugoslavia)* (Beograd: Izdanje "Službenog list FNRJ," 1958).

[20]For a brief but adequate discussion of the Yugoslav system, see: Dušan Jurić and Siniša Pudar, *State and Social System in Yugoslavia* (Beograd: Jugoslavija, 1960); and Aleksandar Jovanović, *Društveno-političko uredjenje FNRJ (Socio-Political System FPRY)* (Beograd: Rad, 1958).

administrative and political functions in the executive arm were theoretically separated. As it turned out, however, this distinction between politics and administration proved operationally unfeasible.

Similar institutional arrangements were also repeated at the republic level of government. Two other territorial divisions were found below the republic level—the district and the commune. The function of the former was rather strictly limited to the political, whereas the latter assumed responsibility for the economic as well as the political supervision of its territory.[21] For example, the people's committee of a commune could decide in large part how accumulated profits within its confines might be allocated for expenditure (whether to build a new enterprise, improve the commune roads, and so forth). Each commune as well as each district elected its people's committee; the structure of these committees paralleled the federal People's Assembly—namely, two chambers one of which represented producers. During this period of thaw, the significant institutional innovation was the functional or economic-based representation provided by the Council of Producers. This innovation can be interpreted as giving an expression to the idea of worker self-management on the political level.

Consistent with the emphasis upon democratizing the environment, special privileges of Party members

[21]For a discussion of the commune system, see: Jack C. Fisher, "The Yugoslav Commune," *World Politics,* XVI (April, 1964), 418–41; Jovan Djordjević, "Le Self-gouvernement local ou le Système communal de la Yougoslavie," *Le régime . . . Yougoslavie,* pp. 102–39; and Jovanović, *Socio-Political System FPRY,* pp. 245–89; see also: Borislav T. Blagojević, ed., "The Local Government," *Collection of Yugoslav Laws,* II (Beograd: Institute of Comparative Law, 1962).

in 1950 were severely curtailed. For example, individuals other than Party members became increasingly eligible for and successful in holding public office. Until 1952 and the Sixth Congress, however, the Party continued to play the classical Marxist or Soviet-style role of directing nearly all political and social life. Despite the resolutions of the Fifth Congress on the Cominform dispute, the Party still tended to emphasize its orthodoxy and to remain well centralized. In the words of Ranković, its statutes were "a copy of the statutes of the Soviet Communist Party."[22] Major changes in party structure and function occurred at the Sixth Congress in 1952, primarily involving a basic decentralization. One effect was that local Party secretaries were ordered to give up many of their positions as heads of local governmental bodies. In addition, Party functionaries in republics were given more authority and autonomy to determine Party stands in their regions than had previously been the case. Designated anew the League of Communists of Yugoslavia, the Party would no longer be "the immediate operational guide and directive-giver neither in economic nor in government and social life." On the contrary, it must contribute mainly through "its own political and ideological activity" and by working "in all organizations, agencies and institutions for adoption of its line and standpoint, or standpoints of its individual members."[23] Generally, the League would limit its function to political education and the setting of

[22]*Politika,* November 9, 1952.

[23]*VI kongres komunističke partije Jugoslavije (Saveza komunista Jugoslavije) 2–7 Novembra 1952, Stenografske beleške (VI Congress of the Communist Party of Yugoslavia [League of Communists of Yugoslavia] 2–7 November 1952, Stenographic Reports),* p. 427.

basic guidelines, whereas other institutions would be charged with the more immediate problems of direction and control. Coupled with decentralization, membership in the League was made somewhat easier to obtain, although special privileges, as mentioned above, had been curtailed.[24] In addition, the old People's Front was now designated the Socialist Alliance; this mass organization was expected to become more involved in aspects of social direction and control previously assumed by the Party. To assure co-ordination and ideological unity, the leadership of the League and that of the Alliance were essentially one and the same.

By 1953 most Yugoslav leaders had become painfully aware that the League might have loosened things up too rapidly. Accordingly, Edvard Kardelj, a leading Yugoslav theorist, warned that League members must not abandon their leadership over the masses; he noted a tendency for members to lose themselves in the Alliance and to leave nominations to "the wild movement of events."[25] In June, 1953, the Brioni Plenum attempted to slow up disintegrative processes by tightening discipline in the League of Communists. Consequently, the League began to expel some of its members, a process that, after the Djilas affair, rapidly accelerated. By June, 1956, party membership declined to 635,984—its lowest point since 1950—as compared to a high of 779,382 recorded for June, 1952.[26] Not only did League membership drop, but a marked decline in

[24]For extensive material on party discussions relating to the role of League members during the proceedings of the Sixth Congress, see: *VI Congress CPY (LCY)*.

[25]*Borba,* September 19, 1953.

[26]George W. Hoffman and Fred W. Neal, *Yugoslavia and the New Communism* (New York: Twentieth Century Fund, 1962), p. 197.

party life and activity also became apparent. The communist leadership had perhaps allowed things to move too quickly and too early toward the realization of a new vision. Tragedy of course marks any such period of rapid change, and so Djilas became the sacrifice to somewhat incautious liberalization.

Over-all, the Yugoslav economy indicated some important gains as compared to earlier periods, despite economic boycott by communist party countries. To a significant degree Yugoslav success was of course due to aid received from the United States at a rather crucial time—namely, it helped Yugoslavia overcome the immediate crisis. First of all, let us examine agriculture; here the Yugoslav emphasis tended to move away from the earlier strong pressure for collectivization (see Table 7). Accordingly, by March, 1953, peasants were allowed to withdraw from work co-operatives with a restitution of land and equipment that they had originally contributed.[27] As a result, we find that land volume within collective farms dropped from a high of 2,422,000 hectares in 1951 to 382,000 by 1956; in contrast, the private farm sector jumped from 9,188,000 to 10,921,000 hectares between these same years.[28] Despite a severe drought in 1952 as well as continued Soviet belligerency, the indices of agricultural production maintained about the same level (or increased slightly) as compared to the 1948 index.[29] Because Yugoslavia

[27]For the government decree dealing with property rights and the status of peasant work co-operatives, see: "Uredba o imovinskim odnosima i reorganizaciji seljačkih radnih zadruga od 30 Marta 1953" ("Regulation on Property Relations and Reorganization of Peasant Work Cooperatives of 30 March 1953"), Law no. 83, *Službeni list FNRJ (Official Gazette FPRY)*, IX, 14 (March 31, 1953), 145–50.

[28]*Statistical Yearbook, 1958*, p. 111.

[29]*Statistical Yearbook, 1962*, p. 107.

returned to a modified private farm economy, and because of the continued pressure from the Communist Bloc, the help of the West was crucial during these transitional years to buy the time necessary for making adjustments.

If we consider the industrial sector alone, we find somewhat more impressive gains during this period, particularly in light of the Soviet boycott. As discussed above, soon after World War II the Yugoslavs succeeded in nationalizing nearly the entire industrial sector of the economy. But the Yugoslav experiment with decentralization and worker self-management was bound to create certain new problems of adjustment and co-ordination of effort. The basic economic task was to generate an environment of competition stressing somewhat modified "capitalist" principles of supply and demand to be tempered and guided, however, by the gentle hand of centralized state authority;[30] any such experiment as this, necessitating extensive structural changes in the Yugoslav system, of course could not be realized without significant costs. Consequently, the period between 1949 and 1952 indicated little progress, if any at all, with the index of industrial production ($1939 = 100$) dropping from 167.4 to 164.6 during this time. However, by 1956 industrial production had risen to 266.5 reflecting, first, a partial normalization of relations with Soviet Bloc countries and, second, an adjustment by the Yugoslavs to a system of socialist competitive enterprises (see Table 6). Basic industries, such as electrical energy, coal and oil, and various

[30]For an exposition of these "capitalist principles" and their application in a socialist society, see: Boris Kidrić, "From State Socialism to Economic Democracy," *Yugoslav Review*, I (February, 1952); and B. Jelić, "Le Système économique Yougoslave," *Le régime . . . Yougoslavie*, pp. 18–22.

metals, also showed important advances.[31] Having braved the storms of political ostracism and socioeconomic experimentation, the Yugoslav system displayed a self-sufficiency that surprised many, and certainly most of all the leaders of the Soviet Union.

The Yugoslav situation during this period can best be defined as one of social experimentation. No guarantees existed that the workers' councils, the communes, or the system of socialist competitive enterprises were going to work out. Whatever the forces might have been that moved the Yugoslav system toward decentralization—the ingrained Yugoslav tradition of localism, the fear of a burgeoning state bureaucracy, an unflinching ideological commitment to "true" Marxism, or a simple reaction to Soviet political domination—the fact remains that by 1956 the necessary basic adjustments had been made by the Yugoslavs. It also became clear by this time that the Yugoslav economy, despite its allegedly heretical Marxist forms, could survive without the buttressing and the succor of Communist Bloc countries. Soon, in fact, Yugoslav institutional innovations were making themselves felt in other socialist states as well, including among them the Soviet Union itself.

Involvement in Two Worlds

The Yugoslav integrative pattern for this period showed movement away from the East toward closer affiliation with Western states. Coupled with Yugoslav disillusionment with its big Soviet brother, a strong

[31]For example, between 1948 and 1956 the production of electrical energy increased from 2,061 million to 5,048 million kilowatt hours. *Statistical Yearbook, 1962*, p. 142.

emphasis was placed upon "peaceful coexistence" and trade with the West. The Yugoslavs came to feel that a country's system was its own business, and that revolution should not (and, indeed, could not) be exported as one might export Russian caviar. This position might be interpreted by some as indicating a certain "softness on capitalism," a condition which did not have its unwarranted appeals to Western observers; consequently, this period saw an unexpected diplomatic intimacy develop between the United States and communist Yugoslavia. Furthermore, the noncommittal attitude of the Yugoslavs found strong adherents among new, underdeveloped states. In turn, this opened the way for Yugoslav leadership of a power bloc defined as neutralist which threatened a strictly bipolar world. For the most part, the Soviet Union could only stand aside and watch the bold defiance and even arrogance of its former satellite.

Had the Soviets anticipated the response by the United States to Yugoslav difficulties, one wonders if they would have so abruptly cast the Yugoslavs out of the club. The nearly immediate result of the Soviet-Yugoslav split was to bring the United States into the drama as savior of the oppressed; Yugoslav defiance of the Soviet "bully" also appealed to the American's image of himself as champion of the underdog. Millions of dollars in economic and technical assistance, in addition to military advisory missions and other military aid, followed this appeal.[32] The role of the United States as benefactor was firmly established by 1950, with Tito requesting and being granted aid from

[32]For a useful examination of details involved in United States assistance to Yugoslavia between 1950 and 1959, see: Hoffman and Neal, *Yugoslavia and the New Communism,* pp. 347–54.

the United States. Several important results followed from this new "unholy alliance." First, it served notice on the Soviet Union that satellite states do not simply disintegrate when deprived of its support. Second, it allowed resolution of certain Balkan problems involving the West—namely, the Trieste issue and Yugoslav meddling in Greece. Third, it illuminated the fact that Western, nonideological appeals could be heard by even the more dedicated Marxists. And, fourth, it pointed up the possibilities of conflict among and the nonalignment of communist-based systems. The pressures, both economic and military, exerted by the Communist Bloc were thus effectively wasted; moreover, the power tactics employed threatened to force Yugoslavia even further into the Western orbit. Accordingly, as early as 1954 a new Soviet policy toward Yugoslavia began to become apparent.

Soviet belligerency and economic boycott encouraged Yugoslavia to seek regional security arrangements. Historically, the Yugoslav pattern had been to attempt to develop a Balkan power base, whether in the form of an entente or a federation. The first Yugoslav step in creating this power base involved signing a Treaty of Friendship and Co-operation in February, 1953, with Turkey and Greece.[33] Co-operation was to be limited to nonmilitary—that is, primarily economic and cultural—aspects; military co-operation, however, was

[33]Državni sekretarijat za inostrane poslove (State Secretariat of Foreign Affairs), "Ugovor o prijateljstvu i saradnji izmedju FNRJ, Kraljevine Grčke i Republike Turske od 28 Februara 1953" ("Agreement of Friendship and Cooperation between FPRY, Kingdom of Greece, and Republic of Turkey of 28 February 1953"), Medjunarodni ugovor FNRJ (International Agreements FPRY) (Beograd, 1953), no. 3.

established a year later with the signing of the Ba
Pact.[34] The parties to this agreement (Yugosla
Greece, and Turkey) guaranteed assistance if any sigi.a-
tory were subject to attack by another state. The United
States also hoped the Pact would help to bring Yugoslav forces into some working relationship with NATO.
If the United States diplomatic corps was somewhat
elated about the Balkan Pact, the Soviet reaction was
equally (if not even more so) one of astonishment and
apprehension. As a result of the Balkan Pact coupled
with Soviet internal political developments, the Soviet
Union began to move toward a rapprochement with
Yugoslavia: economic trade restrictions were lifted,
Danube Commission countries ceased their harass-
ment, and feelers went out from Moscow hoping for a
stepped-up trade program. In general, the Soviet Union
displaced power tactics with diplomatic courtship as
the means for bringing Yugoslavia back into the fold.
Despite his formal commitments, Tito soon began to
disavow military obligations under the Balkan Pact
and, specifically, the American presumption that it
associated Yugoslavia in some way with NATO. Easing
of tensions between Yugoslavia and the Soviet Union
culminated in May, 1955, with the Khrushchev-Bulga-
nin visit to Belgrade. Upon his arrival, Khrushchev
made an unusually warm and conciliatory speech; he
in effect acknowledged the success of the Yugoslavs in
going it alone and in expanding their relations with

[34]"Zakon o ratifikaciji dopunskog sporazuma izmedju FNRJ,
Kraljevine Grčke i Republike Turske" ("Law on the Ratification
of the Supplementary Agreement between FPRY, Kingdom of
Greece, and Republic of Turkey"), *Službeni list FNRJ (Official
Gazette FPRY)* (Beograd, 1954), Dodatak (Supplement) I.

nonaligned states.[35] The speech marks the end of Soviet attempts to isolate Yugoslavia, although the old relations of dependency were never to return.

The new Soviet attitude permitted the Yugoslavs more fully to assume their new role—namely, that of mediator between two worlds. The Khrushchev proclamations on "peaceful coexistence" sat well with Yugoslav notions that the West was not irrevocably aggressive; the two worlds could co-operate with one another if they were so inclined. Furthermore, the Yugoslav peacemaking role had also generated contacts with like-minded uncommitted leaders, such as Nehru of India and U Nu of Burma. After having made official visits and having toured several of these neutral states, Tito decided to convene a conference of nonaligned states at Belgrade and assume thereby the unofficial leadership of a third, neutralist bloc. Understandably, therefore, the Yugoslavs began to take pride in their role as mediator between two worlds, a role that they felt not only contributed to world peace but also proclaimed the integrity of small states.

All these developments worked to establish a phenomenon that came to be known as Titoism—namely, a commitment to a socialist system but nonalignment politically. The "national" brand of communism had its expected appeals to other satellite states as well; in fact, it generated not wholly unpredictable unrest among satellite states as, for example, with the Poznan riots. The height of "national communism" among satellites appeared to culminate with the 1956 Hungarian revolution and its military suppression by the

[35]Robert Bass and Elizabeth Marbury, eds., *The Soviet-Yugoslav Controversy, 1948–1958: A Documentary Record* (New York: Prospect Books, 1959), p. 51.

Soviet Union. Following the Hungarian revolution, relations with Yugoslavia again deteriorated (and they did so rather quickly), with the Soviet press attacking both Tito and "national communism."[36] Earlier the Yugoslavs had themselves strongly condemned the harsh Soviet measures taken in Hungary; despite a reluctant approval of intervention, they felt that the whole episode had disgraced international socialism.[37] On the other hand, the cooling of relations strengthened the independent Yugoslav position on "active coexistence" and the role it wanted to play as the nonpartisan bridge between East and West.[38] Attacks by the Soviet press in addition to blatant economic pressures not only slowed down the process of rapprochement but also postponed agreement on trade relations; understandably, they made Yugoslav leaders noticeably more hesitant about any further involvement with the Soviet Union. From the Yugoslav standpoint, the new "crisis" situation with the Soviet Union was comparable to the one they had confronted immediately after the Cominform split.[39] The Yugoslav policy of avoiding firm alliances became essential owing to Soviet economic pressures and what was seen as violation of agreements for political expediency.

The widening scope of Yugoslav relations became apparent as reflected by certain "hard" indices and, primarily, its trade pattern (see Table 8). These indicators reveal a shifting of trade from communist party

[36]*Pravda,* November 23, 1956.

[37]Bass and Marbury, *The Soviet-Yugoslav Controversy,* pp. 75–86.

[38]Aleš Bebler, "Jugoslavija i Evropa" ("Yugoslavia and Europe"), *Medjunarodna politika (International Politics)* (September 16, 1956), pp. 5–6.

[39]*Borba,* February 27, 1957.

countries to both the Western and the nonaligned world. We find, therefore, that by 1953 the volume of Yugoslav imports from the United States including foreign aid accounted for 34.4 per cent of its total import trade; in addition, the United States purchased 13.9 per cent of total Yugoslav goods exported abroad. These trade figures involving the United States were much higher than analogous figures for 1948 and the prewar period. A similar change was suggested by fig-ures defining West German trade with Yugoslavia, which involved 17.4 per cent and 16.6 per cent of Yugo-slav volume for imports and exports respectively.[40] The unfavorable Yugoslav trade balance suggested by United States data was offset in part by favorable trade balances with nonaligned states. In addition, the data show that more trade was carried on with the neutralist bloc after the Soviet-Yugoslav split than before; accord-ingly, by 1957 Yugoslav trade with Afro-Asia accounted for 8.1 per cent of its imports and 12.5 per cent of its total exports.[41] By 1957 and with rapprochement well on its way, the volume of Soviet-Yugoslav trade in-creased slightly, although it was never to resume the impressive pace revealed by 1948 figures. Based upon 1957 data, Yugoslavia even held a somewhat favorable trade balance with the Soviet Union itself.[42] On the whole, these data indicate sharp departures from earlier Yugoslav economic dependence upon communist party

[40]*Statistical Yearbook, 1955,* p. 212.

[41]*Statistical Yearbook, 1962,* p. 188. For a general discussion of Yugoslav trade patterns for this period, see: Hasan Brkić, "Naši ekonomski odnosi sa inostranstvom" ("Our Economic Relations Abroad"), *Economic Policy FPRY,* pp. 425–36.

[42]Trade figures show that in 1957 Yugoslav exports to the Soviet Union accounted for 13.2 per cent of the total, while its imports were 10.4 per cent of its volume. In addition, Yugoslav exports to the Soviet Union exceeded exports to the United States by 4.6 percentage points. *Statistical Yearbook, 1962,* p. 188.

,tates, in addition to an unquestionable trend toward leveloping and expanding Western markets. They also reveal the need for Yugoslavia to expand its trade with the less developed world as a means of reducing its unfavorable trade balance.

Other factors that also give evidence of orientation toward the Western world include, first of all, the tourist trade and, secondly, book translations. Accordingly, although in 1948 Czechoslovakia sent 22,258 tourists to Yugoslavia, in 1953 the number was too small to record; however, by 1957 Czechoslovak tourists numbered 11,522, representing an increase that showed the impact of the rapprochement (see Table 9). To contrast with this, between the years 1948 and 1953 West German tourism in Yugoslavia increased from 3,318 to 56,898; similarly, tourist figures involving American visitors to Yugoslavia show a rise from 868 to 17,892 between these years.[43] We can discover similar trends by examining book translations based upon the language of origin. Accordingly, for 1949 we find that 458 books were translated from the Russian, for 1952 there were 126, and for 1955, only 43 such books. In contrast to this, although for 1949 only 39 books were translated from the English, for 1952 there were 235, and for 1955 we find 146 such translations.[44] In conjunction with Western-oriented patterns of trade, cultural and literary interest also seemed to move somewhat toward the West. Generally, we can see intensified efforts to develop and expand economic as well as cultural ties with the noncommunist world.

We find in the period after 1949 an attempt by Yugo-

[43]*Ibid.*, pp. 116–17.
[44]*Index Translationum: International Bibliography of Translations* (Paris: UNESCO), 1953, no. 5, pp. 385–409; and 1956, no. 7, pp. 517–34.

slavia to arrive at a new, more balanced pattern of integration. Having been rejected and excommunicated by its comrade states, it was forced to seek association and help in what had been alien territory. The immediate result was the development of a relatively independent Yugoslav posture in its relations with other states. Furthermore, it established useful ties with noncommunist countries (Western as well as nonaligned), providing the foundation for an independent foreign policy. The attempt by the Soviet Union to boycott, and therefore to destroy, the Yugoslav regime effectively backfired; indeed, it had the unanticipated result of creating an effective working model of "national communism" that posed a threat to a Soviet-dominated Bloc. If Tito could succeed in his defiance of Moscow, what was to preclude other satellite leaders from doing the same? The willingness of Western states to open their doors to communist rebels, in addition to the Soviet desire for reconciliation, permitted the Yugoslavs the added luxury of operating in two worlds. Furthermore, they learned quickly that adroit playing of the Western diplomatic game best maximized benefits from both camps.

The catalyst to Yugoslav institutional and ideological innovation undoubtedly had its source in the Cominform split. Stripped of the authority and security provided by a pristine and historically tried Soviet model, the Yugoslavs had to develop a new basis of legitimacy for their experimental "independent road." Furthermore, it became necessary to give concrete institutional form to the Yugoslav critique of Soviet centralized bureaucracy, which culminated in the workers' council system as the empirical counterpart of a theory of decentralization. The enterprises were to be handed over to the producers where, as any proper Marxist should know, they rightfully belonged. The force of this new attitude also affected other aspects of the system, such as producer representation in political bodies, loosening strict party discipline, and reversing the process of collectivization. Certainly the most significant impact of these changes was the opening of doors to the Western world. Observers in Western countries liked the crude but genuine decentralizing tendencies they saw at work in Yugoslavia; they also praised the sometimes indiscreet but always sincere bravado of the young state in its relations with the Soviet Union. As a result, both financial help and respectability were forthcoming from Western states; understandably, this pattern of Yugoslav behavior had its appeals to nonaligned countries as well. The new Yugoslav posture was ultimately to permit Yugoslavia to define a unique role for itself as a socialist state in world affairs. It could serve as the avenue (or at least the symbol) by which the two opposing worlds might seek intelligent solution to pressing issues. In addition, Yugoslavia provided the model for "national communism" as well as for worker self-management, which other socialist states might wish to adopt. More recent developments seemed to have vindicated the Yugoslav positions on both these counts and to have justified the American diplomatic gamble. Even the Soviet Union has attempted to institute socialist competitive enterprise, while the force and frequency of autonomy among communist party states has become increasingly apparent.

5: THE STAGE OF MAINTAINING A VIABLE EQUILIBRIUM

Urban-Rural Balance

Perhaps the terms most suitable for describing the more recent Yugoslav situation are those of *balance* and adjustment. Earlier we saw that Yugoslav disaffection with the Communist Bloc resulted in the cultivation of ties with Western countries. In the period of concern here (1957–63) we discover a shift backward toward a renewal of profitable ties with communist party states, without however abandoning fruitful relations that had been developed with the West. On the whole, the Yugoslav policy of formal diplomatic nonalignment was continued during this period. With respect to beliefs and values, the partisan war experience persisted as a basis for country-wide solidarity, buttressed also by a certain pride taken by Yugoslavs in the relative success of their system. The basic Marxist innovations of the preceding stage were also somewhat more fully articulated; in addition, some ideological issues were clarified and sharpened as a result of the Sino-Soviet dispute. Internally, the most salient feature was the persistent exodus from the village into the town and the city, in conjunction with official pressures exerted

toward an industrialized and modernized system. Contributions to Yugoslav economy emanating from it
Western ties contrasted sharply to continued ideological orientation (albeit, in a modified form) toward the
communist world.

The basic census data for this period show a continued and steady population growth in Yugoslavia. According to the most recent census, Yugoslav population
stood at 18,549,291 in 1961, which represented an increase of about 1,600,000 over 1953 census figures. I
current trends are projected, by 1970 Yugoslav population should exceed 20,000,000. In absolute figures
the largest population gains were recorded for the
Serbs (7,806,000) and the Croats (4,294,000), the forme
increasing by 740,000 and the latter by 318,000 ove
the 1953 census (see Table 1). From a percentage stand
point, the Albanian minority increased more rapidl
than any other ethnic group in Yugoslavia; there wer
21 per cent more Albanians in 1961 than there were i
1953, with a total of 914,000 recorded representing
about 5 per cent of the total Yugoslav population. The
Macedonian national group also displayed rapid growth
with a 17 per cent increase in population between thes
years. Both of these figures should be contrasted with
an over-all Yugoslav percentage increase of 9.5 over it
1953 population. On the other hand, for the Magyars
who represent the other large non-Slavic minority, pop
ulation growth was almost imperceptible. If we com
bine the various national minorities (Albanians, Mag
yars, Turks, Slovaks, Rumanians, Bulgars, Italians
Czechs, and "others"), we can account for 10.4 per cen
of the total population of Yugoslavia.[1] This figure indi-

[1]Savezni zavod za statistiku (Federal Bureau of Statistics), Sta
tistički godišnjak SFRJ, 1964 (Statistical Yearbook SFRY, 1964
(Beograd, 1964), p. 84.

cates a significant nearly two point percentage reduction of "national minority" elements if compared to data derived from the 1953 census.

Two special "nonethnic" census groupings—namely, the *muslimani* and the undeclared Yugoslavs—taken together account for 1,290,000 inhabitants or about 7 per cent of the population. What characterizes these elements is an apparent reluctance or unwillingness to identify with any *specific* ethnic or national group. Generally, this may well suggest a continued trend toward identification with a more inclusive designation (that is, "Yugoslav") as against the narrower Serb or Croat. Any such tendency would be expected to accelerate as communication and transportation facilities improve and as movement from agricultural and historic locales toward cities and industrial centers continues. In conjunction with this, we find in official circles the expression of a "Yugoslav socialist patriotism" as the legitimate form of nationalistic sentiment.

Often we find that the correlates of a modernizing society include lower birth rates as well as lower death rates. Bearing out this thesis, Yugoslavia in 1961 recorded a death rate of 9.0 and a birth rate of 22.6 per thousand inhabitants, with both figures being significantly lower than 1953 indices (see Table 4). Understandably, the natural increase also dropped from 16.0 to 13.6 per thousand between 1953 and the 1961 census.[2] These indices were even lower by 1963, with a birth rate of 21.4, a death rate of 8.9, and a natural increase of 12.5.[3] Not surprisingly, the underdeveloped areas of Yugoslavia displayed considerably higher rates of natural increase than shown by the country-wide

[2]*Ibid.*, pp. 82–83.
[3]Federal Institute for Statistics, *Yugoslavia, 1958–1964: Statistical Data* (Beograd, n.d.), pp. 20–21.

index. Accordingly, based upon 1963 figures, we find a natural increase of 28.9 for Kosovo-Metohija, 21.4 for Bosnia-Hercegovina, 19.6 for Macedonia, and 19.5 for Montenegro. If we compare 1957 data for Kosovo-Metohija alone, we discover a lower natural increase than that for 1963, a phenomenon that runs counter to the country-wide trend. The apparent "population explosion" in Kosovo-Metohija results from significant reductions in death rate (1957 = 17.5 and 1963 = 12.0) which is found in conjunction with a continuing high birth rate (1957 = 39.1 and 1963 = 40.9). A provoking and instructive contrast to Kosovo-Metohija may be found in the Vojvodina; here we find a natural increase of only 6.1 per thousand which represents the lowest such figure in all Yugoslavia. Furthermore, the Vojvodina for 1963 registered a relatively high death rate (9.2) as against the lowest birth rate (15.3) in the country.[4] These data tend to reflect the wide gap that separates the more advanced northern regions of Yugoslavia from the less developed south. As a result, the Yugoslav regime has consciously pursued a policy of accelerated investment in these less advanced southern regions. Generally, we can expect rapid growth of population to continue in these southern regions, especially in Kosovo-Metohija and Macedonia. On the other hand, the population of the more advanced northern sections of the country (for example, Slovenia and the Vojvodina) should continue to increase at rather slow rates.

Perhaps the most "revolutionary" force in Yugoslavia continues to be rapid urbanization of society. Just prior to World War II slightly over 75 per cent of the Yugoslav populace were dependent upon agriculture

[4]*Statistical Yearbook, 1964,* pp. 360–61.

for their sustenance and livelihood. By 1961 this figure had dropped to just under 50 per cent of the total population.[5] Figures show that although 10,105,587 persons in 1953 operated within the agricultural sector, by 1961 this had declined to 9,169,764 persons. In contrast, although in 1953 the industrial sector included 1,140,606 persons, by 1961 this had increased to 2,191,256 or twice the earlier figure (see Table 5). Regional contrasts relating to proportion of the population involved in agriculture are also instructive. Accordingly, in more advanced Slovenia we find only 30.9 per cent of the population tied to agricultural pursuits, whereas less developed Kosovo-Metohija still identified 64.1 per cent of its population as agrarian.[6] Data on Yugoslav cities perhaps best reflect the general migration of people toward urban centers. This becomes clear not just for the larger cities, such as Belgrade (598,346), Zagreb (457,499), or Sarajevo (198,419), but also for towns that serve as industrial and market centers within the various communes. For example, the town of Nikšić in Montenegro nearly doubled its population between 1953 and 1961 (from 10,323 to 20,166), as did also Titograd. On the whole, the towns and cities have grown more rapidly in the less developed central and southern regions of Yugoslavia than they have in the north. For example, although in 1953 Ljubljana (Slovenia) had been the fourth largest city of Yugoslavia, by 1961 it was overtaken by Skopje (Macedonia), which had increased 40.6 per cent over 1953 census fig-

[5]*Ibid.*, p. 85. For a useful discussion of these population shifts and their effect upon the Yugoslav economy, see: Branko Horvat, "The Characteristics of Yugoslav Economic Development," *Socialist Thought and Practice* (1961), no. 1, pp. 83–97.

[6]*Statistical Yearbook, 1964*, pp. 351–53.

ures.[7] Any projection of trends for Yugoslavia would of course have to specify continued high rates of migration toward urban and industrial centers. This movement should be reflected in growth rates in provincial cities as well as in commune towns.

Other factors relevant to changing demographic structure in Yugoslavia include skill levels and literacy. The Yugoslavs have taken considerable pride in the reduction of illiteracy, which before World War II had characterized about half the population of the country. By 1953 the illiteracy rate of Yugoslavia had been reduced to 25.4 per cent and by 1961 to 19.7 per cent of the total population.[8] Regionally, however, these literacy figures tended to vary considerably; therefore, although in Slovenia only 1.8 per cent of the population were illiterate, in Bosnia-Hercegovina the statistics encompassed 32.5 per cent of the populace, most of whom were older people. Recognizing the need of both skills and literacy for an industrialized society, the Yugoslavs continue to press for higher educational achievement in all sectors of the country.[9] Statistics indicate that the number of students in "basic schools" for 1962–63 doubled that for the 1938–39 school year (from 1,470,000 to 2,960,000). Furthermore, attendance at "technical and other special schools" for 1962–63 (158,339) was fifteen times greater than for 1938–39 and threefold that indicated by 1956–57 figures. Finally, if we compare 1962–63 data with those

[7]*Ibid.*, p. 636.

[8]*Yugoslavia, 1958–1964*, p. 23.

[9]For a recent examination of the development and nature of the Yugoslav educational system, see: Radoljub Jemuović, *Education in Yugoslavia* (Beograd: Medjunarodna politika, 1964). Specifically on the Yugoslav universities and their operation, see: Marijan Filipović, *Higher Education in Yugoslavia* (Beograd: Jugoslavija Publishing House, 1962).

for 1938–39, we find that the number of students involved in "higher education" has increased tenfold.[10] The Yugoslav drive for modernization requires development of a professional and technical class that only an improved educational system can provide. Only more education can create the requisites for transforming a traditional and peasant-based society into a modern industrialized system.

Demographic structure in Yugoslavia increasingly betrays certain salient modernizing trends. Most significant perhaps is the development of a professional and a skilled class, with the not unanticipated by-product of a rapidly declining peasant culture. We find that both literacy rates and skills have risen impressively over the years in Yugoslavia, which contributes to this development. In addition, the old conflict-provoking ethnic ties (Serb, Croat, and so forth) give some evidence of being less "irrational" and less binding, with more individuals thereby willing to think of themselves quite simply as individuals operating within a broad Yugoslav context. The pattern of religious affiliation has most probably changed little from that indicated by 1953 data, although a slight increase in the "nonbeliever" and the Moslem categories seems to be indicated. Generally, demographic trends in Yugoslavia began to approximate those that are somewhat characteristic of Western industrialized systems.

Ideological Factors

Having weathered problems and controversy arising from independent socialism, the Yugoslavs began to export their experience in the form of Titoist ideology.

[10]*Statistical Yearbook, 1964,* p. 311; see also: Jemuović, *Education in Yugoslavia,* pp. 26–28; and, Filipović, *Higher Education in Yugoslavia,* pp. 16–18.

Both the nonaligned and the communist worlds felt that something might be adopted from the Yugoslav experiment with new socialist forms. Images and tales surrounding partisan sacrifice and victory continued to provide the emotional matrix that bound the Yugoslav people together and that united them against challenges from the outside. Both cultural and historical identification, as well as economic ties, with the Western world also tended to be further intensified during this period. Most important perhaps was a conviction that existing Yugoslav leadership had done a rather good job of solving old ethnic divisions and reducing strife. In these terms, it might well be that in part the efficiency of the government itself created a basis for confidence in and loyalty to constituted authority. On the whole, the Yugoslavs believed that their nation state was moving forward, with each element in the system making its unique contribution to Yugoslav progress.

Several factors in Yugoslavia continued to work toward a somewhat less dogmatic belief system. First, increasing personal and economic contact with the West (as reflected in impressive tourist figures in recent years) further broke down the isolation of the Yugoslav people. Second, the self-image Yugoslavs had of themselves as successful organizers of an independent bloc, in addition to their role as brokers between the Soviet Union and the United States, generated a measure of pride in the achievement of the communist regime.[11]

[11]Josip Broz Tito, "Non-alignment—Universal Movement for Peace," *Socialist Thought and Practice* (1963), no. 12, pp. 4–5. Useful selections on Yugoslav theory extracted from the writings of Tito, Kardelj, and Ranković can be found in Hamdija Pozderac and Bratislav Petković, eds., *O socijalističkoj demokratiji u Jugoslaviji (On Socialist Democracy in Yugoslavia)* (Beograd: Kultura, 1961).

Third, Yugoslav living standards had risen sharply through 1960 and, since then, have continued to maintain a more modest but still a persistent increase. This social improvement coupled with a "truce" with the thick-skinned peasantry has enabled the regime to broaden its base of authority and to jettison the rigid centralism of the earlier so-called administrative period. Finally, a significant degree of liberalization has taken place in aspects of political life which do not directly affect leading personalities and the central authority. This liberalization has created an important safety valve and permits ever wider and healthier criticism within a framework also acceptable to the regime. Although hard-core ideological issues in the strict sense could not be discussed, criticism of methods of administration and planning has tended to be quite extensive. All these factors suggest an environment (one generating personal security and confidence in the regime) within which a limited dialogue relating to beliefs could be effectively carried on.

During the earlier "thaw" period Yugoslav theory had already stressed the decreasing role of the League of Communists. The League's removal of pressure upon elements in Yugoslav society was explicitly recognized by theorists as a new phase in socialist development. We find this expressed in the formula that a newly transformed base—namely, social self-administration—existed in Yugoslav society and, therefore, that a certain relaxation could be permitted. Logically, this follows, since one of the effects of a new social experience would be the transformation of superstructure; stated somewhat differently, new and more appropriate political forms must be generated in light of the new social experience. In practice, this meant that the League no longer felt a need to press strenuously for affirmation of its basic goals; Yugoslav society as a whole no longer needed to be constantly and forcibly mobilized by League elements.[12] This would suggest that the process of the last twenty years in Yugoslavia was considered by many as being irreversible, which would seem to betray a certain security taken by Yugoslav leadership in their socialistic achievements.[13] Appropriately, the 1958 program states that the League "will gradually, in the long run, disappear with the developing and strengthening of ever more inclusive forms of immediate socialist democracy."[14] This statement would lead one to believe that the disappearing act of the League has already begun, with the direct social administration of Yugoslav society by the working people being imminent. As we shall see later, however, more recent happenings suggest a reaffirmation of the League as a vigorous and active guide of developments in Yugoslavia.

In addition to invoking the old and worn images of partisan experiences, the new myth stressing the independent Yugoslav road to socialism was reconsolidated. Both these myths continued to re-enforce the

[12]See: Prvoslav Ralić, "Samoupravljane i društvena kritika" ("Self-Management and Social Criticism"), *Socijalizam* (1963), no. 4, pp. 145–49.

[13]Najdan Pašić, "The Self-Contradictions of State Capitalism and Circumstances of the Class Struggle," *Socialist Thought and Practice* (1962), no. 6, pp. 63–87.

[14]*Program Saveza komunista Jugoslavije (Program of the League of Communists of Yugoslavia)* (Beograd: Kultura, 1958), p. 219. See also: *Yugoslavia's Way: The Program of the League of Communists of Yugoslavia* (New York: All Nations Press, 1958); and, for a more recent analysis of the role of the League and its members, "The Third Plenum of the Central Committee of the League of Communists of Yugoslavia," *Socialist Thought and Practice* (1962), no. 5, pp. 101–02.

strength and authority of the communist regime, thereby giving a credibility to its moral claim to leadership over diverse Yugoslav elements. Like any mythical system, the Yugoslav expression was derived from a basic truth that has been somewhat exaggerated and transformed to achieve specific effects. One can question, for example, whether in the true sense more liberties existed in Yugoslavia than in either Poland or Hungary; but Yugoslav "freedom" was still a logical derivative of the basic myth of the independent road. The myth dramatizing an "independent road" has without question been significant and even crucial to the success of the Yugoslav experiment. In fact, it has served the necessary dual function of consolidating forces at home while withstanding pressures from abroad. Another function of the "independent road" has been to disarm Western critics by pointing to liberalization policies as well as to decentralization in Yugoslavia.[15] Both these factors—namely, partisan wartime experience and the independent road to socialism —will most likely continue indefinitely as the underlying matrix of Yugoslav state authority.

The belief in "social self-administration" of the Yugoslav system leading to disappearance of state machinery continued to be stressed. However, a somewhat more cautious attitude was soon adopted, to wit, a state of anarchy must not be tolerated in the name of decentralization and local initiative. The regime must struggle against two dangers: (1) "against the tendency of an anarchistic underestimation of the role of the

[15]Moma Grujić, "Poslednji kongresi Kommunističkih partija u socijalističkim zemljama" ("Recent Congresses of Communist Parties in Socialist Countries"), *Socijalizam* (1963), no. 1, pp. 75–84.

state"; and (2) "against the tendency of transforming the state into an all-embracing social force."[16] Accordingly, the function of the state becomes that of a regulator or a ballast between, on the one hand, too much local autonomy and, on the other, too much centralized bureaucracy. Despite this admonition against the dangers of either extreme, socialist competitive enterprise and decentralization remained at the heart of Yugoslav Marxist theory.

The Yugoslav theorist continued to testify to the desirable long-term effects of inner contradiction as the motive force behind progress. Consistent with this, Tito could proclaim that "the world develops through contradictions."[17] Acknowledgment of contradictions was perhaps symptomatic of a rather sensitive and deep problem—namely, allowing some degree of local autonomy in planning but yet recognizing the need for centralized federal control. The basic conflict, therefore, was still "between the orientation towards the development of self-government, on the one hand, and the conservative-bureaucratic orientation, on the other."[18] The League of Communists still remained the crucial unifying force through which a minimal level of country-wide co-operation could be guaranteed. This

[16]*Program of the League of Communists of Yugoslavia,* pp. 115–16.

[17]"Press Conference by Josip Broz Tito, Secretary General of the League of Communists of Yugoslavia," *Review of International Affairs,* XV (December 20, 1964), 5. See also the 1958 program on the role of contradiction in social development in: *Program of the League of Communists of Yugoslavia,* pp. 140–42.

[18]Veljko Vlahović, "The League of Communists of Yugoslavia and Ideological Trends," and Edvard Kardelj, "Distribution of the Product of Socially Organized Work and Social Planning," both in *Review of International Affairs,* XV (December 20, 1964), 33, 24–28, resp.

meant that League members had to be ideologically active, for "Socialist Democracy also presupposes the broadest influence of the League in all fields of life."[19] What had been lost for co-ordinated effort by a genuine institutional decentralization is regained in part by encouraging greater activism by party members.

Consistent with his reverence for the function of contradictions, the Yugoslav theorist must not choose finally between incompatible· assertions. Accordingly, although it is recognized that political forms generally stem from socioeconomic relations and material conditions, no specific form springs automatically from such relations or conditions since man can choose between better or worse solutions to problems.[20] Both voluntaristic and deterministic aspects are thereby given their due, illustrating the intimate link between theory and practice in Marxist thought. Similarly, contemporary Yugoslav society must become more homogeneous while at the same time becoming more complicated; a kind of unity emerges from an only apparent diversity. We find a "growing complexity in the sociopolitical system parallel with the simultaneous increase of homogeneity in society."[21] This would suggest a

[19]Vlahović, "The League of Communists," p. 34. Elaborating this thesis in somewhat more graphic form, Jovan Djordjević asserts that "the role of the League of Communists is not only to express socialist awareness but to be a factor of development of this awareness, without which there is no achievement of future development." "Basic Characteristics of the New Constitution of the Socialist Federal Republic of Yugoslavia," *Two Decades of Socialist Yugoslavia* (Belgrade: Medjunarodna Politika, 1964), p. 41.

[20]For instance, see: Petar Stambolić, "On Forms of the Political System and the Organization of the Federation," *Socialist Thought and Practice* (1963), no. 11, pp. 89–112.

[21]*Ibid.*, p. 102.

displacement of a complexity (as well as a conflict) grounded in ethnic division by one derived from commune-based economic interest and enterprise competition. Rather than ethnic strife and bloodshed, one will find only socialist competition and progress, with the choice as to desirability being clearly evident. Contradictions had also become apparent in what has been termed "economic nationalism" by some observers of the Yugoslav scene.[22] If ethnic rivalries have somewhat subsided in Yugoslavia, regional animosities still persist that, at times, take the form of bitter economic competition. But most intelligent Yugoslavs recognized that problems and tensions arising from regional economic competition are simply one of the costs of industrial progress.

Most important perhaps has been the impact of Titoist innovations upon other communist party systems. In this respect, claims of influence might be made which include a developing "socialist competition" in the Soviet Union as well as the more adventurous polycentrism of the Italians.[23] Also significant here of course are the images of Yugoslav communists held by other parties. Currently, their closest ties appear to be with the Italian Communist Party, which represents the most liberal of such movements. The Yugoslavs have also displayed strong approval of Poland and Hungary (and, particularly, those satellite states with liberal leanings) among the various communist regimes of Eastern Europe.[24] The Yugoslav League of Commu-

[22]For example, see: J. F. Brown, "Eastern Europe," *Survey: A Journal of Slavic and East European Studies* (January, 1965), pp. 82–86.

[23]Marijana Janković "Deseti kongres Komunističke partije Italije" ("The Tenth Congress of the Communist Party of Italy"), *Socijalizam* (1963), no. 1, pp. 85–97.

[24]Grujić, "Recent Congresses," p. 83.

nists has also taken pride in its role as intermediary between the communist parties of Eastern Europe and the socialist parties of the Western world. Accordingly, we can observe close ties and lively dialogue between the Norwegian Social Democratic Party and the League of Communists through the instrument of the Socialist Alliance. In general, the Yugoslavs have tried to justify their system in terms acceptable to Western-style socialists; as a result, they tend to stress the workers' councils and decentralization as being fundamental to the Yugoslav road to socialism. This Yugoslav approach would appear to reveal a somewhat more "democratic" (as well as a more popular) appeal than what can be offered by the more devoted communist parties of Eastern Europe. In addition, because of the widespread appeal of the Yugoslav road to socialism, the other communist party systems of Eastern Europe have been inclined to develop more liberal socialist forms of their own.

The Yugoslav brand of Marxism has maintained what might be termed a rather healthy contempt for theory. Consistent with this, Kardelj has asserted that a socialist system "cannot be reduced merely to general proclamations of socialism." In fact, any system whatever must respond "to the blows of the everyday pressure of practicism."[25] The Yugoslavs have also proclaimed that they must continue to build a "social community" with roots firmly embedded in extensive worker participation in local communes. Furthermore, persistence of contradiction will continue to require endless processes of change and improvement within Yugoslavia. Certain integrative forces of course serve

[25]Edvard Kardelj, "Constitutional Foundations of Socialist Social-Economic Relations and Social Self-Government," *Socialist Thought and Practice* (1963), no. 11, p. 9.

to co-ordinate efforts within the system; these include intelligent geographic distribution of leadership as well as a party persistent both in its efficiency and in its ethnic blindness. In addition, a popular confidence in the communist regime's efficiency and its successes in developing Yugoslav industry has provided a more convincing basis for state authority and obligation. Finally, it becomes clear that Yugoslav ideological innovations have had a significant impact upon developments in other socialist states.

Institutions and Economy

Yugoslav sociopolitical forms tended to reflect attempts at realizing direct socialist democracy. The leadership of the country, feeling that the state apparatus could in fact wither away, continued to institute forms thought to be conducive to that end. Consequently, a much greater emphasis was placed upon the autonomous role of the commune and workers' councils as concrete expressions of social self-administration. The state must begin to wither away by mass participation at the commune and enterprise level. Concurrently, the Yugoslav system of representation has taken on a strongly functional or interest-group aspect, indicating an economically based system of social order rather than a politically based one. Yugoslav theory anticipates that formal political relations and the state apparatus would ultimately become obsolete when a fully producer-operated society has been realized. On the other hand, integrative factors as counterforces to decentralization and direct socialist democracy continued to involve the League of Communists, economic associations, and the trade union system. Finally, rather significant advances in Yugoslav economy (particularly, the availability of consumer goods) were evident, even suggesting a certain affluence if compared with previous experience. On the whole, the Yugoslav social and political system appeared to move toward a fulfillment of the goals of the independent road.

The office of the President of the Socialist Federal Republic of Yugoslavia has taken on a somewhat more significant role than previously.[26] Combining parliamentary with American presidential elements, the President (namely, Tito) in effect appoints his ministers or cabinet as he is "empowered to entrust one of the deputies of the Federal Chamber with drafting the list of members for the Federal Executive Council."[27] The President also exercises a "veto power" over all decrees issued by the Federal Executive Council, in addition to serving as commander-in-chief of the armed forces. The more formal, ceremonial function of the President as head of state infuses the office with a charismatic potential, consistent with the role that Tito has developed for himself within the Yugoslav system. To contrast with the job held by Tito, the top administrative or ministerial office is that of President of the Federal Executive Council. In effect, the Presidency of the Yugoslav Republic is a prestigious office that in a sense stands above possible factional or intraparty strife.

[26]This top position in Yugoslavia should not be confused with the presidency of the Federal Assembly held during this period by Edvard Kardelj, or with that of the presidency of the Federal Executive Council filled by Petar Stambolić.

[27]Stambolić, "On Forms of the Political System," p. 106; see also: *Ustav Socijalističke Federativne Republike Jugoslavije (Constitution of the Socialist Federal Republic of Yugoslavia)* (Zagreb: Narodne novine, 1963); and *The Constitution of the Socialist Federal Republic of Yugoslavia* (Beograd: Secretariat for Information of FEC, 1963), Article 216.

With Tito at the helm the office symbolizes Yugoslav unity achieved through the force of strong personal leadership.

The basic and greatly stressed principle underlying the Yugoslav system of government is that of unity. Outspoken in their rejection of the divisibility of sovereign power, the Yugoslavs consider that sovereignty must remain undivided since the people and their representatives must be as one.[28] As we saw above, even the earlier experiment with division of administrative and political organs had been abandoned. On the other hand, the nature of a decentralized system, coupled with application of the federal principle, would seem to generate something akin to a checks and balances system or at least a plurality of affiliations and power centers. Therefore with continued decentralization a variety or plurality of socioeconomic forces might well bring pressure upon and influence the federal state authority. Conditions for a pluralistically disposed socialist order might be generated by continued Yugoslav emphasis upon local autonomy and functional representation. In part at least, this would seem to controvert Yugoslav claims for the growing unity of their over-all system, although it is also argued that a tolerance of diversity functions as a condition for unity.

Yugoslavia has moved toward a system of representation focusing upon socioeconomic groups or "chambers of working communities." In addition to the general Economic Chamber within the Federal Assembly, we find specific chambers devoted to education and cul-

[28]Stambolić, "On Forms of the Political System," p. 111; and, Edvard Kardelj, *The New Yugoslav Federal Assembly* (Belgrade: Federal Assembly Series, 1964), p. 5.

ture, social welfare and health, and organization-politics.[29] The Federal Chamber, which represents no specific working community but rather the citizenry in general, and the Chamber of Nationalities were carried over from the earlier system. Basic to the new system is the attempt to distribute representation among so-called self-governing groups or working communities in Yugoslav society.[30] Theoretically, this can be viewed as an attempt to establish interest-group or functional representation and to institutionalize potential group conflict in the system.

The new constitution adopted in 1963 has also explicitly formalized the *indirect* system of election or representation. Under new electoral methods the commune assemblies (formerly, people's committees) select members of district, republic, and federal assemblies from lists nominated at voters' meetings. More specifically, members of the Federal Chamber are elected by both commune assemblies and by electors in constituencies, whereas those in the various functional chambers (economic, education and culture, and so forth) are selected by the commune assemblies alone.[31] Formerly election to the Council of Producers discriminated against the peasantry since representation was based upon social product determined in a manner to undervalue agricultural commodities. By way of contrast, the present electoral system takes into account the *actual* working population, although only those peas-

---

[29]*Constitution SFRY*, Article 165; and Kardelj, *The New Yugoslav Federal Assembly*, pp. 33–35.

[30]Stambolić, "On the Forms of the Political System," p. 92.

[31]*Constitution SFRY*, Article 169; and Stambolić, "On the Forms of the Political System," pp. 94–95.

ants who are members of co-operatives may vote for delegates to producers' assemblies.[32] The effect (at least in part) has been to reduce biases that existed in the former system of representation favoring the proletariat at the expense of the peasantry.

As for mass participation in politics, the trend has been increasingly toward multiperson nominations. Generally, with the exception of a few seats reserved for top party personnel, the local members of the League are obliged to show not simply that they are loyal and hard working, but also that they have some genuine popularity among the multitude. What is more, Yugoslav law now forbids the re-election of candidates to successive terms of office. Electoral procedures call for the convocation of voters' committees that for the most part operate on a "town meeting" principle in which active dialogue is stressed. Significantly, recent years have seen a growing number of cases in which more than one candidate was submitted by voters' committees to regional nominating assemblies. In addition, the frequency of multiple-candidate lists tends to increase as one moves from the federal to the commune level of election. Generally, three rather significant factors—indirect election, functional representation, and multiple candidates—point to important changes in the Yugoslav political system.

Local political arrangements in Yugoslavia reflect two major processes of development—namely, industrialization and agricultural displacement. Industrial development has tended to result in a rapidly expanding work force that must draw upon the peasantry for its members. On the whole, rural social structure has

[32]Joze Vilfan, "Discussion," *Socialist Thought and Practice* (1962), nos. 7–8, pp. 86–93.

maintained basic elements bequeathed from the pre-entry stage, despite co-operative-style institutions and basic pressures toward change. The coming of industry into rural areas has required extensive participation by members of peasant families, involving either commuting to nearby industrial towns or employment in locally established plants.[33] Therefore, the peasant community has experienced crosscurrents of social and economic pressures which bring their traditional values into conflict with their role as industrial workers. The viability of the Yugoslav system will depend largely upon how effectively local and traditional structures will adapt to changes necessary for industrialization in the future.

A mass-related local authority implemented the policies of a country-wide mobilizing government as well as administering the affairs of the commune. To realize social self-management and direct democracy, wide participation among the populace has of course been encouraged. Accordingly, an impressive variety of committees, commissions, citizens' councils, public boards, and other bodies now exist for this purpose. These are buttressed by voters' meetings, which provide the citizen with an increasingly larger role in local government and public affairs. These local citizens' bodies also tend to move toward somewhat open discussion as long as fundamentals are left alone—that is, as long as no direct challenge to central authority and socialist foundations result. On the whole, these extensive arenas of mass participation provide effective mechanisms for political education and governmental experience for the citizen.

[33]Branko Horvat, "The Characteristics of Yugoslav Economic Development," *Socialist Thought and Practice* (1961), no. 1, pp. 83–97.

For the Yugoslav system the most important local body, and the one that assumes more and more real power, continues to be the commune. The assembly and council of the commune function as key governmental and administrative bodies for regulation of socioeconomic activity. These communes also exercise wide powers of taxation and co-ordinate plans of the workers' councils for enterprises under their territorial jurisdiction. Through a bicameral system (a producers' chamber and a broader citizens' one) the commune exerts socioeconomic pressure upon workers' councils to consider commune or social needs as well as those of the enterprise itself.[34] In addition to its economic or planning function, the commune provides municipal services and is in charge of administering social services to its region. Over the years communes have become fewer in number but larger in size; from 1,193 in 1958 they were reduced to 577 by 1964.[35] This development—namely, fewer but larger communes—simply magnifies the greater role that the commune now plays in the Yugoslav system. On the whole, the commune has increasingly been taking over from the district many local governmental and administrative functions affecting the day-to-day life of citizens. In addition, greater decision-making power for investment has been left to these local governmental units.[36] In terms of

[34]Kardelj, "Constitutional Foundations," pp. 7–55; see also: *Constitution SFRY*, Articles 69, 76, and 77.

[35]*Yugoslavia, 1958–1964*, p. 15. A detailed description of Yugoslav communes as of 1962 is provided in: Milan Mesarić, ed., *Komune i privreda Jugoslavije (Communes and Economy in Yugoslavia)*, 2 vols. (Zagreb: Orbis, 1962).

[36]For statistical evidence in support of this generalization, see: George W. Hoffman and Fred W. Neal, *Yugoslavia and the New Communism* (New York: Twentieth Century Fund, 1962), p. 250.

official ideology, the commune together with the workers' council represents the "grass roots" institution of decentralization which gives Yugoslav socialism its somewhat unique character.

Arising out of the Djilas affair and early in this period, a slight tightening of discipline and control by the League of Communists had occurred. This took the form of introducing a large number of party "actifs" into governmental departments in conjunction with establishing party schools for training new and better cadres. A major new recruiting campaign was also launched combined with extensive use of cadres in the army and local government. This new party approach meant a slight and brief revival of more direct involvement by League members in local governmental operations. By many this was interpreted to mean somewhat more open roles for party units in "suggesting" measures to mass organizations and local bodies. However, as usually seems to be the case, processes unleashed by liberalizing trends are difficult to reverse. Fairly widespread resentment of renewed tightening of controls resulted in some strikes, and perhaps even contributed to the major strike that occurred at Trbovlje in Slovenia. In February, 1958, the central committee in a letter to League organizations denounced "dictatorial methods," special privileges, and the practice of favoritism.[37] Consequently, after the Seventh Congress in 1958 a somewhat less direct and open role of the League of Communists was stressed once again.

Some attempt was made at the Seventh Congress to achieve a new balanced role for the League of Communists. Although formally the controlling role of the

[37]For this problem, see: *Komunist,* February 28, 1958.

League was to go unchallenged, in practice the Socialist Alliance was to assume greater significance in the Yugoslav system. As things developed, local governmental bodies and workers' councils in enterprises also kept increasing in prestige and in authority. Greater stress upon professional competence, upon legal and formal channels, and upon socialist legality, all tended to circumscribe the League of Communists as the primary factor in Yugoslav political life. Although the League tried to involve large numbers of people in its lectures, classes, and schools (that is, in political education), there was evidence that much of this met with "good humor" and even apathy among the young. Generally the stress upon governmental channels and the Socialist Alliance encouraged the view that the League had become a sort of "honor society." As a result, formal governmental institutions at nearly all levels have tended to assume both more importance and more legitimacy.[38] More recently, however, Yugoslav theorists have again observed and pointed to a certain laxity in enthusiasm of League members for active work in local organizations.[39] The trend over the last few years has thus involved a slight tightening of

[38]Vojin Hadžistević, "Menjane društvenog položaja radničke klase Jugoslavije" ("Transformation of the Social Situation of the Working Class in Yugoslavia"), *Socijalizam* (1963), nos. 5–6, pp. 44–46.

[39]Lazar Koliševski, "Basic Features of the New Statute of the League of Communists of Yugoslavia," *Review of International Affairs,* XV (December 20, 1964), 37. For a recent history of the Yugoslav party, see: Radoljub Čolaković, Dragoslav Janković, and Pero Morača, eds., *Pregled istorije Saveza kommunista Jugoslavije (Survey of the History of the League of Communists of Yugoslavia)* (Beograd: Institut za izučavanje radničkog pokreta, 1963).

discipline and a prodding of party members to become more active.

In recent years the Yugoslav economic system has given indications of a degree of self-sufficiency and (one might hazard) even affluence. Consumer goods have become more available with more people also being able to afford and enjoy them. Statistical indicators show that personal consumption for Yugoslavs in 1963 had increased by 97 per cent over the 1958 level.[40] We find that Yugoslavs were producing and buying more electric ranges, refrigerators, televisions, motorcycles, radios, automobiles, and so forth, than ever before. For example, data show that 43,113 motorcycles were produced in 1963 as compared to 8,202 in 1958. As for the purchase of motorcycles, the 1963/1958 consumer index stood at 314.0, showing a marked rise between these years.[41] As well as desirous economic benefits for the Yugoslav system, these consumer patterns have their effects upon breaking down regional loyalties and peasant culture since they create a more geographically mobile population. A related development has been the improvement and expansion of the road systems and general travel conditions in Yugoslavia. Both the industrial and the agricultural index of production

[40]*Yugoslavia, 1958–1964*, p. 79.

[41]In addition, refrigerator production in 1963 stood at 122,246 as compared to 7,414 in 1958; automobiles produced during these years were 20,923 and 2,936 respectively. *Yugoslavia, 1958–1964*, pp. 45, 87. Similarly, radio purchases by 1962 included 2,040,000 units as compared to 710,694, according to 1956 figures. *Statistical Yearbook, 1960*, p. 287; and Federal Institute for Statistics, *Statistical Pocketbook of Yugoslavia, 1964* (Beograd, 1964), p. 100. The 1963/1958 consumer index for televisions was 756.0, for electric ranges 643.0, and for refrigerators 742.0—all, of course, showing strong advances. *Yugoslavia, 1958–1964*, p. 87.

have continued to indicate rather steady upward trends (see Tables 6 and 7). Measured with 1952 set at 100.0, Yugoslav industrial production was able to generate a 363.0 index by 1963.[42] Agricultural production has also risen, although not as impressively as has industry; measured also with 1952 as the base, agricultural output in 1963 stood at the 218.0 level.[43] With population steadily moving toward industrial centers, the share of national product attributed to industry and services should also continue to increase.

Since 1956 the Yugoslav government has tried to increase the role of its General-Purpose Agricultural Co-operatives.[44] By joining such co-operatives the peasant receives the benefits of modern equipment, administration, and expert advice, while still retaining legal ownership of his small plot of land. These voluntary co-operatives have for the most part been well received with fairly large-scale involvement on the part of the peasants. Furthermore, they represent an educational arena for exposing the small peasant landholder to the basic principles of a progressive socialist society. These co-operatives have also been quite successful in increas-

[42]*Statistical Yearbook, 1964,* p. 177. A useful analysis of indices of production for various items of manufacture—such as energy, metallurgy, and so forth—is provided by Drago Krndija, *Industrializacija Jugoslavije (The Industrialization of Yugoslavia)* (Sarajevo: Ekonomski institut univerziteta, u Sarajevu, 1961), pp. 106–26.

[43]*Statistical Yearbook, 1964,* p. 142. However, it is necessary to point out that 1952 was a "bad year" for Yugoslav agriculture. With the agricultural index for 1930–39 at 104, agricultural output for 1961 stands at only the 147 level, a somewhat less impressive gain than that suggested if 1952 were used as the base. *Statistical Yearbook, 1962,* p. 107.

[44]Edvard Kardelj, *Problems of the Socialist Policy in the Countryside* (Beograd: Yugoslavia, 1960), pp. 31–34.

ing the general level of agricultural output, since their level of productivity usually outstrips the private farm sector. A factor that continues to grow in importance for the over-all Yugoslav economy has been the burgeoning tourist trade of recent years. Between 1956 and 1963 the number of foreign tourists visiting Yugoslavia increased from 393,803 to 1,754,663 for the given season (see Table 9). Most of these tourists come from Western countries and in particular from Austria and West Germany; in 1963 these two countries provided Yugoslavia with about 45 per cent of its tourist trade.[45] Such continuous and intensive contact with the West through tourism would of course be expected to have its impact upon the nature of Yugoslav society. On the whole, the Yugoslav economy has shown important advances, particularly in industrial and consumer goods production. Combined with adroit Yugoslav maneuvering in a bipolar world, these developments suggest a certain level of national self-sufficiency.

The apparent contradiction between a decentralized socioeconomic system, on the one hand, and effectively centralized political control, on the other, will most likely continue in the future. The question remains whether socioeconomic trends toward more local autonomy and more "technocratic efficiency" will not also require the development of different (namely, nonpolitical) recentralizing mechanisms. In fact, the Yugoslavs indicate that they are becoming more involved in seeking such new instruments of co-ordination. Certainly, the over-all trend appears to be toward more authority and power being centered in duly constituted public organs of government and functional groups in

[45]*Statistical Yearbook, 1964,* pp. 260–61.

place of the League. A significant Yugoslav innovation for this period was the institutionalizing and expansion of economic-group conflict through a system of producer (or functional) representation. The commune as the pristine, model institution of direct socialist democracy should continue to be stressed, with districts most likely of decreasing importance, largely because they never constituted a viable socioeconomic unit. Finally, steady advances in Yugoslav economy, and particularly in industry and consumer goods, make the self-sufficiency of Yugoslavia a somewhat more attainable goal.

Balanced Integration Pattern

In recent years the Yugoslav pattern of relationships with other states has tended to become stabilized. After spending a considerable period of time striving to define a role for itself in world affairs, Yugoslavia in this period moves with a not unwarranted confidence in diplomatic circles. In addition to maintaining a cautious distance from both power blocs, Yugoslavia could now also lay claims to leadership status in its own right —namely, in relation to nonaligned countries. Rather than develop embarrassingly close ties with either East or West, the Yugoslavs have tried to maintain a somewhat diffuse pattern of relationships. As a result, both the United States and the Soviet Union have condemned Tito for what appeared to them to be opportunistic moves in world affairs. But when a state can raise the ire of both East and West, then it seems that a measure of independence as well as influence has been achieved.

A key point in developing Soviet-Yugoslav rapprochement was Khrushchev's speech before the Twentieth

Party Congress and, in general, the de-Stalinization program in the Soviet Union.[46] Particularly satisfying to the Yugoslavs was Khrushchev's reiteration of what were seen as Titoist principles in setting forth the new Soviet approach to world problems. Rapprochement between these states involved a renewal of economic relations, in addition to *de jure* recognition by Yugoslavia in October, 1957, of East Germany. At this juncture Tito also agreed to attend (although only as a "fraternal guest") a meeting of communist parties held in Moscow in November, 1957, that celebrated the fortieth anniversary of the Soviet revolution. In response to what appeared to be growing Soviet-Yugoslav reconciliation, the United States hardened its own line and threatened to terminate aid to Yugoslavia.[47] This change in United States policy was also affected by an earlier Yugoslav refusal to go along with a United Nations censure of Soviet repression of the Hungarian revolt. In typically heroic but somewhat naïve Balkan fashion the Yugoslavs reacted by telling the United States to go ahead and cut off aid if it so chose. The Yugoslavs, however, declined to sign the official declaration that emanated from the Moscow conference, although their presence was still hailed by the Soviets as indication of a renewal of close ties.[48]

Growing Soviet-Yugoslav rapprochement was sharply set back by vitriolic attacks by the Chinese Communist

[46]For the text of Khrushchev's initial condemnation of Stalin, see: "The Crimes of the Stalin Era: Special Report to the 20th Party Congress of the Communist Party of the Soviet Union by Nikita S. Khrushchev," *The New Leader* (Supplement), n.d. [1956].

[47]*New York Times,* November 18, 1957.

[48]Hoffman and Neal, *Yugoslavia and the New Communism,* p. 447.

Party, for whom the Yugoslav League symbolized chronically feared "revisionist" currents in the Soviet Union. Accordingly, at the Seventh Congress of the Yugoslav League the Soviet ambassador walked out, followed devotedly by other communist delegations with the single exception of the Poles. With the arrival of Spring, 1958, therefore, Soviet-Yugoslav relations were again at a rather low ebb; threats emanated from Moscow which indicated that Soviet aid to Yugoslavia might well be halted. By June, 1958, even the Polish government joined the attack, and the Yugoslavs were once more isolated from the communist world. With renewed Soviet-Yugoslav disaffection by October, 1958, the United States again saw fit to extend new loans to Yugoslavia.

Rising tensions between the Soviet Union and Yugoslavia were further underscored by the 1960 Moscow statement by communist leaders. By implication it attacked the Yugoslavs for their foreign policy opportunism and their domestic adventurism, in addition to making some concessions to the Chinese communist position.[49] In their reply, Yugoslav spokesmen stressed that any confidence that the Yugoslav people might have had in the possibility of renewed normal relations with Communist Bloc states was severely shaken.[50] As a result of the disaffection, the Yugoslavs intensified their general efforts in two directions. First of all, they hoped to develop closer ties with underdeveloped and non-aligned countries in order to consolidate a third force

[49]See the 1960 Moscow conference statement in: G. F. Hudson, Richard Lowenthall, and Roderick MacFarquhar, *The Sino-Soviet Dispute* (New York: Frederick A. Praeger, 1961), pp. 202–03.

[50]Veljko Vlahović, "Korak nazad" ("A Step Backward"), *Komunist,* February 25, 1961.

in world politics. Second, they attempted to generate positive relations with communist parties in noncommunist states, as for example with the Italians, who also expressed interest in closer ties with the League. The Yugoslavs began an ideological counter-offensive, focusing upon the Chinese Communist Party as the progenitor of inflexible Marxist dogma as well as a proponent of what was seen as a reckless posture toward the Western world.[51] The Yugoslavs also saw the conference of nonaligned states which took place in Belgrade in Summer, 1961, as the foundation of a possible third bloc. These nonaligned states were expected to act as a bridge between the two major power blocs; they would also constitute an independent force for world peace.[52] Since the Yugoslavs had feared definite commitments to either power bloc, the sensible alternative was to develop a third power base with other states who also shared such fears. Relations with Western countries (particularly trade relations) continued to expand and improve while the League of Communists also tried to intensify contact with social democratic parties.

Somewhat more recently, a stabilization of relations between Yugoslavia and its neighbor communist party states has been developing. The fact that other communist party states have themselves begun to show greater independence and are developing more liberal domestic programs has contributed to this relaxation and normalization. From their side, the Yugoslavs maintain that they want to seek and develop individual

[51]The Yugoslav position is clearly explicated by: Edvard Kardelj, *War and Socialism* (New York: McGraw-Hill, 1960).

[52]For documents relating to the Belgrade meeting, see: *Conference of Heads of State or Government of Non-aligned Countries* (Beograd: Jugoslavija, 1961).

relations on strictly bilateral terms with their neighbors, rather than dealing with an entire bloc as such.[53] As a result of this bilateral approach, Yugoslav relations with Rumania, Bulgaria, and Czechoslovakia could by 1963 be defined as "normal," whereas in the cases of Hungary and Poland they could even be termed "cordial." In brief, we find Yugoslavia placing heavy emphasis upon the need for countries such as itself to remain outside and independent of either system of alliances.[54] Only in this way, the Yugoslavs argue, can a relatively small and weak country like Yugoslavia make positive contributions toward mobilizing an effective force for world peace. Countries representing a third power bloc must be unalterably hostile to all military alliances, be committed to a stronger United Nations, and act as a bridge between states in the Soviet and Western blocs. More recently (October, 1964) the Cairo conference of nonaligned states has reaffirmed these basic principles as well as conferring joint leadership of the third bloc upon Tito and Nasser.[55] It may also be argued that growing liberal trends among Soviet satellite states give these independent Yugoslav innovations and aberrations a certain rationale or "I told you so" aspect. Although clearly free from awkward military alliances and economic bloc entanglements, Yugoslavia remains a self-proclaimed com-

[53]Veljko Vlahović, "Conditions Have Been Established for Closer Cooperation Between the League of Communists and Communist and Workers' Parties in Other Countries," *Socialist Thought and Practice* (1963), no. 12, pp. 59–68.

[54]Josip Broz Tito, "Non-alignment—Universal Movement for Peace," *Socialist Thought and Practice* (1963), no. 12, pp. 5–17.

[55]For documentation on the Cairo Conference, see: "Second Conference of Non-aligned Countries," *Review of International Affairs,* vol. XV (November 5, 1964).

munist state with a certain heroic appeal to communist as well as noncommunist countries. Furthermore, the Yugoslavs themselves take considerable national pride in their role as leaders of an international movement for peace.[56] Generally, with respect to their domestic model the Yugoslavs have exerted strong influence upon Hungary and Poland, whereas in foreign policy their impact has been mainly upon the noncommunist world. The main partners of Yugoslavia in terms of foreign policy commitment generally include the Italian Communist Party and the underdeveloped nations.

One important measure of the degree of interstate integration is found in trade patterns. If we assume trade (expressed in dinars) to be a more or less valid measure of integration, we are forced to conclude that Yugoslavia maintains a quite effectively balanced pattern (see Table 8). Data show that by 1961 Yugoslav trade with the Soviet Union had decreased as compared to earlier figures, involving only 3.8 per cent in imports and 8.9 per cent in exports of total value of Yugoslav trade. In contrast to this, trade between the United States and Yugoslavia accounted for 19.5 per cent of Yugoslav imports and 6.4 per cent of its exports; this pattern also reveals an unfavorable trade balance for Yugoslavia with the United States. In the same year, the Yugoslav trade pattern with Afro-Asian

[56]Josip Broz Tito, "Uloga Saveza komunista u daljoj izgradnji socijalističkih društvenih odnosa i aktuelni problemi u medjunarodnom radničkom pokretu i borbi za mir i socijalizam u svetu" ("The Role of the League of Communists in the Further Construction of Socialist Social Relations and Current Problems in the International Workers Movement and the Struggle for Peace and Socialism in the World"), *Osmi kongress Saveza komunista Jugoslavije (Eighth Congress of the League of Communists of Yugoslavia)* (Beograd: Komunist, 1964), p. 9.

131

countries indicated a volume of 7.2 per cent and 14.5 per cent for imports and exports respectively. Two countries that consistently maintain extensive trade relations with Yugoslavia are Italy and West Germany; together these accounted for 30.1 per cent of Yugoslav imports and 22.4 per cent of its exports in 1961.[57] On the whole, more current data also confirm these basic trade patterns, although 1963 figures show a definite increase in Soviet-Yugoslav trade. The recent trade volume between these states, however, still fails to attain levels indicated by 1957 data just prior to re-newed Soviet-Yugoslav disaffection in 1958. Based upon 1963 figures, imports from the Soviet Union made up 6.8 per cent and its exports 10.8 per cent of the total volume of Yugoslav trade, which represents an increase of about two percentage points over 1961. In comparison, the amount of United States trade with Yugoslavia has dropped slightly to 17.6 per cent and 5.8 per cent respectively for imports and exports, based upon 1963 data.[58] In more recent years the volume of Yugoslav trade with other communist East European states has also tended to increase. Furthermore, Yugo-slavia has been granted the status of "observer" in the proceedings of the East European trade community de-fined as the Council for Mutual Economic Assistance. Nevertheless, the primary Yugoslav markets have con-tinued to be Western states, particularly Italy and West Germany, while Yugoslavia also sits as an "ob-server" in the Organization for Economic Co-operation and Development. Generally, these data suggest a dif-fuse trade pattern for Yugoslavia with a minimal over-balancing toward any one group of states. In addition,

[57]*Statistical Yearbook, 1962*, p. 188.
[58]*Statistical Yearbook, 1964*, p. 233.

the Yugoslav trade balance during this period continued to be unfavorable (that is, considerably more imports than exports), although larger amounts of manufactured goods were being exported.

Salient developments in foreign relations give further evidence of a balanced Yugoslav pattern of integration. First of all, we find that Yugoslavia has been producing and assembling Fiat automobiles through an international agreement with the Italian firm. The interstate co-operative effort that brought relief to victims of the Skopje earthquake included United States' contributions of large contingents of personnel and funds to the salvage operation. In addition, more recently both the Ford Foundation area studies and the Fulbright program have been expanded to include Yugoslavia, with the latter occasioning the visit of Senator Fulbright to that country. Finally, the Yugoslavs have entertained bids from international firms for rebuilding the city of Skopje, a procedure fully compatible with their dedication to the market principle for economic problems. All these events would of course suggest rather healthy relations with the West. From the other side, however, we also find that ties with the communist party states of Eastern Europe during this time were expanded and strengthened. As mentioned above, Yugoslavia now participates in the COMECON trade bloc as an "observer" in addition to making specific bilateral trade and other agreements with individual communist states. For example, the Yugoslavs have been engaged with Rumania in joint efforts to harness the hydroelectric potential of the Danube at the Iron Gates. On the whole, statistical data indicate that Yugoslav trade with Communist Bloc countries has also been on the upswing in more recent years. The Yugoslavs feel that both the United States and the Soviet Union honestly seek intelligent accommodation, although in Marxist terms they still tend to divide the world into progressive and reactionary forces.[59] This pattern suggests that Yugoslavia has been inclined to pursue those relations, irrespective of the nature of the bloc, that are seen as working toward the maximizing of Yugoslav national interest.

A balanced pattern of relationship has served Yugoslavia as a necessary factor for its survival as an independent state. Yugoslav leaders know full well that to be too far removed from, or too entangled with, either major power bloc is to court disaster. Tactically and metaphorically, one must avoid political starvation as well as political suffocation. Accordingly, the solution must be found in those elements in the arena of world politics which are beholden to neither major world power. Likely candidates to help achieve this balancing or intermediating role are of course the United Nations and the nonaligned world. Yugoslav strategy has been precisely to develop these two instruments as a guarantee of (or, at least, a buttress to) its own state autonomy. The United Nations and the nonaligned bloc, therefore, have been strategically used to keep both the United States and the Soviet Union at a convenient distance. On the other hand, the Yugoslavs have not been so taken with their pride as to refuse any benefits in the form of trade or assistance offered by these states.

The Yugoslav situation during this period can perhaps best be defined as one of dynamic strategic accommodation. Its internal sociopolitical situation has grad-

[59]Tito, "The Role of the League of Communists," p. 8.

ually been modified to gain a degree of tolerance and respect from both East and West. If the fact that Yugoslavia remains a dedicated Marxist state pleases Moscow, certain other factors (namely, decentralization, "national communism," and a modified market economy) find strong approval in the Western world. Central to this period are the continued industrialization and urbanization of Yugoslav society, and changes in population and belief structure which accompany such development. Displacement of population from small villages to commune towns and large cities has been working toward the demise of long-standing peasant values and traditions. The crucial operative elements central to the Yugoslav fabric of authority include myths depicting partisan war experience as well as a faith in the independent road. Both of these are of course placed within the context of Marxist ideological commitment, buttressed by the communist regime's efficiency in developing industrial capacity and in containing latent ethnic animosity. Generally, Yugoslav political articulation has moved increasingly toward an interest-group or functional system of representation, while developing a presidential office not unlike those found in the Western world. Consistent with the commitment to direct socialist democracy, the commune and the workers' council have become the primary arena for ideological education and sociopolitical experience. On the world scene, Yugoslavia has tended to operate in two worlds for maximizing its national advantage in addition to developing its own power base in association with nonaligned states.

6: RECENT DEVELOPMENTS—
UNCERTAIN TRENDS

Events that have transpired in Yugoslav society since 1964 contain profound implications for accelerated modification in the nature of the system. The major innovation involves the economic reforms legislated in July, 1965, which are only now having some measure of effect upon the country. Another event of significance for Yugoslav society has been the ouster of Ranković and his associates in the Spring of 1966,[1] with the resulting alleged de-emphasis upon the Yugoslav state security service apparatus (the secret police). Still another new item focuses upon the role of the League of Communists, which is best reflected in the declaration by Tito that the League must gradually separate itself from political-administrative affairs. And, finally, the Yugoslav elections of April, 1967, seem to give a radically different cast to the nature of Yugoslav leadership; this change might best be described as putting more stress upon younger, more sophisticated, and better educated men. The several trends noted in earlier chapters—exposure to the West, increased mobility of the populace, intensified modernization, more tolerance of ideological expression, and greater indus-

[1]*New York Times,* July 2, 1966.

trial capability—all continue into the present as viable forces effecting change in the Yugoslav system. Generally speaking, it might even be argued that recent events raise serious questions about the propriety of classifying Yugoslavia as a communist party state.

The extensive regional variation within Yugoslavia still remains as apparent as it was in the past, although the country as a whole seems increasingly to display attributes of a modernized society.[2] Analyses of recent census data suggest that the growth rate for Yugoslavia as a whole in the period 1961–71 will be about 11.3 per cent (as compared to 10.8 per cent for 1953–61) with a projected total population by 1975 of 21,732,000 inhabitants.[3] However, what seems more relevant in this context is the nature and the breakdown of any such population increase. Given the greatly improved medical facilities within Yugoslavia, the population of the country tends on the whole to be getting older. The proportion of individuals in the fifty-and-over group has been increasing over the years, whereas those in the nineteen-and-under category are apparently decreasing in number.[4] Such a trend it seems could well reflect the sophisticated modern urbanite's conviction that a family should have no more than two or perhaps three children. Relevant also to this modernizing process is the extensive migration within Yugoslavia from the countryside to the cities. The data show that larger numbers of Yugoslavs are moving to urban centers as re-

[2]An informative analysis of projected trends in Yugoslav demography is provided by: Milica Sentić and Dušan Brežnik, "Demografska kretanja i projekcije u Jugoslaviji" ("Demographic Change and Projections in Yugoslavia"), *Stanovništva (Population)* (1964), no. 2, esp. pp. 129–39.

[3]Federal Institute of Statistics, *Statistical Pocketbook of Yugoslavia, 1965* (Beograd, 1965), p. 19.

[4]Sentić and Brežnik, "Demographic Change," p. 110.

flected in the actual loss of inhabitants in about half the communes in the country. It should also be noted that the Yugoslav illiteracy rate has diminished to about 15 per cent of the adult population, although with considerable variation indicated among regions (for example, Slovenia as compared to Kosovo-Metohija). Furthermore, the proportion of the Yugoslav populace engaged in manufacturing, commercial, and service forms of industry continues to grow rapidly. Such a trend also has its reflection in the higher index of industrial production (1964 = 691) as well as in the spectacular rise in various catering services owing for the most part to increased tourism.[5] An important byproduct of Yugoslav internal migration touching upon regional integration is the bringing of varied ethnocultural groups into more extensive contact with one another. In this regard, we find for instance that many individuals from Bosnia-Hercegovina have been moving into Slovenia where they now constitute a large sector of the unskilled labor force. Such developments as these suggest that regional integration within Yugoslavia can best be achieved (if at all) with the help of the natural and irresistible play of economic forces.

The demographic trends indicated here for Yugoslavia are characteristic of most countries experiencing rapid economic growth. These modernizing factors include intensified mobility and migration, more skilled workers in industry, an increasingly older population, a reduced death rate, greater mixing and contact among ethnocultural groups, and rising consumer expectations. All these factors combined suggest a number of

[5]Data on "catering turnover" in Yugoslavia show that, while 151,306 million dinars had been spent in 1961, 256,188 million dinars were expended in 1965. *Statistical Pocketbook, 1965,* pp. 51, 78.

implications for Yugoslav political life in general. As already seen, the degree to which modernizing trends exist varies significantly from one region to another within Yugoslavia; consequently, the geographic distribution of state investment in the economy has tended to be a crucial political issue given the clear economic growth differentials. Furthermore, it seems that increased job mobility and widespread migration could signify that a broader cultural and attitudinal consensus might develop within Yugoslavia. These widespread movements of people also mean of course that the many peasants freshly arrived from the countryside can present difficulties as regards assimilation into their new social and economic milieus. Perhaps the most far-reaching effect upon politics will follow from the more politically aware, the increasingly urbane, and the more economically sensitive Yugoslav citizenry that seems to be developing. The Yugoslav regime will, it seems, increasingly have to respond to and honor the demands of a progressively more articulate and wary constituency.

Easily the most interesting development relating to Yugoslav ideology has been the growth of a vital, and even heated, internal debate about the meaning and application of Marxist theory. In 1964 a group of young professors and scholars from the University of Zagreb established a Marxist-based journal of sociopolitical criticism with the title *Praxis*.[6] The relevance of

[6]The first number of *Praxis* appeared in September, 1964, and has been published regularly on a bimonthly basis. An international edition is also published which contains articles written in English, French, and German; the first number of this international edition appeared in January, 1965. This selection of languages by *Praxis* would seem to reveal its strongly cultural orientation toward the Western world.

this journal is found in its outspoken commitment to Marxism, however a Marxism that is grounded in the "young Marx" of all-out criticism, deep concern for alienation, and socialist humanism. As a result, this group of writers has been engaged in running ideological debates with the more traditional and orthodox Marxist in Yugoslavia.[7] As a further consequence, an active dialogue (with a wide range of viewpoints expressed) has been going on in Yugoslavia in recent years, a dialogue that focuses upon the issues of which Marx is the "true Marx" and how his basic works are to be interpreted. Generally, the *Praxis* group holds that Marx was first and foremost a social critic and a socialist humanist; they also maintain that certain institutions may well have to be abandoned (even the one-party system), *if* it can be demonstrated that they violate the humanistic premises of Karl Marx. Here the possibility is suggested that a society can be broadly Marxist with the "working people" in command, but that this need not require an inflexible party dictatorship (either based in a strong personality or in a single social class). In general, the *Praxis* attitude is that a wide range of social forces should be allowed to express their ideological convictions, and that a "loyal opposition" might well form itself and behave in a manner consistent with socialist principles.

A symptom (and perhaps a victim) of this internal Yugoslav process of liberalizing ideological debate is

[7]Top theoreticians of the League of Communists and governmental officials have openly confronted and challenged the validity of the interpretations of the "young Marx" expressed by the *Praxis* group. See for example: Edvard Kardelj, "Notes on Social Criticism in Yugoslavia," *Socialist Thought and Practice* (1965 and 1966), nos. 20 and 21, pp. 3–61 and 3–51 respectively.

found in the so-called Mihajlov case.[8] This young academic argued for, and tried to set up, an "opposition journal" that was designed to be non-Marxist and non-materialist in basic orientation. He pointed out that such an opposition movement within Yugoslavia would be perfectly consistent with the provisions of the new 1963 Yugoslav Constitution. However, from the regime's standpoint, Mihajlov seems to have gone a bit too far (especially in his soliciting of funds abroad), overstepping acceptable limits to ideological diversity, and as a result he has been tried, convicted, and sentenced for behavior injurious to Yugoslav society. It would of course in one sense be an easy matter to condemn the Yugoslav regime for its ideological intolerance in this particular instance. What is far more important, however, is that the Mihajlov case reflects both the obvious potential for, as well as the apparent limits upon, ideological variation within the context of contemporary Yugoslav society.

From a somewhat more official stance, Yugoslav theorists have recently participated in a number of international conferences dealing with the role of Marxism in the modern world. But here also (as domestic developments would suggest) the Yugoslavs have played the

[8]The case arose when Mihajlov circulated a specific proposal challenging the monopoly of the League of Communists on information media and advocating the creation of a movement in opposition to the regime within Yugoslavia. For the full text of this specific proposal, see: Mihajlo Mihajlov, *Elaborat: O mogućnosti osnivanja otvoreno opozicionog štampanog organa u okviru pozitivnih zakonskih propisa SFRJ (A Study: On the Possibility of Establishing an Openly Opposition Published Organ Within the Framework of Positive Legal Regulations of the SFRY)* (Zadar, July 24, 1965); and in English: Mihajlo Mihajlov, *A Historic Proposal* (New York: Freedom House, June 16, 1966).

role of ideological mavericks with a number of the *Praxis* group as participants; they suggest that Marxist theory can no longer be viewed as the exclusive monopoly of communist parties, and that the Marxist pantheon of "theologians" must be expanded beyond the holy trinity of Marx, Engels, and Lenin.[9] Attitudes such as these have made the Yugoslav theorist vulnerable to renewed charges of "revisionism" by communist leaders in most nonparty as well as party states (including a snubbing by the Havana conference on revolution), although in many communist parties there is also evidence to suggest that Yugoslav ideas concerning the interpretation of Marx have had a significant impact. On the whole, this radical Yugoslav posture within the Marxist context has given a new vitality to international dialogue on the proper application of Marxism (taken in its broadest sense) within the modern world. The Yugoslav departure from ideological orthodoxy has, as it were, "shaken up" the communist world and has stimulated creative thought about the utility of Marxist principles to present-day problems.

The experiment in Yugoslavia with the market economy and other presumably Marxist institutional forms has also generated theoretical innovation. It has become clear that, given the system of producer ownership of the means of production, a new concept of property has had to be developed—that of *social property* as opposed either to private or state property.[10] As of the moment the concept still remains quite vague,

[9] A good statement of this general position is provided by: Gajo Petrović, "Marxism versus Stalinism," *Praxis* (Int'l. Edition) (1967), no. 1, pp. 55–69.

[10] Jovan Djordjević, "A Contribution to the Theory of Social Property," *Socialist Thought and Practice* (1966), no. 24, pp. 83–88.

but current Yugoslav experience has at least encouraged attempts at theoretical formulation; the basic implication is that property somehow belongs above all to those individuals who participate *directly* in the processes of social self-administration and enterprise production. Furthermore, the principle of private ownership also seems to be taking on increased legitimacy, with the basic theme that socialism (in the Yugoslav sense) and private ownership do not unavoidably confront one another as incompatible forces.[11] Whether the stress happens to be upon social or private ownership, the basic theme in Yugoslav thought still calls for clear rejection of "state ownership" of property in the Soviet administrative sense.

Certainly a major modification that is suggested in the Yugoslav system relates to the separation of the League from active political power.[12] Although the full implications of any such policy are currently rather uncertain, it does remain consistent with the thesis that the League of Communists provides ideological guidelines *only* and must involve itself less in the direct administration of public affairs. The operational effect of this separation of "party from power" would require that an individual may not hold a position of authority *both* in the League and in the government, although it is expected that governmental officials would for the most part also be members of the League of Communists. The result seems to suggest that the League as a bureaucratic, direct-control instrument would tend to "wither away," with the presumption that the existing

[11]Kiro Hadživasilev, "Fenomen privatne svojine u socijalizmu" ("The Phenomenon of Private Property under Socialism"), *Komunist,* May 5, 1966.

[12]Krste Crvenkovski, "Divorcing the Party from Power," *Socialist Thought and Practice* (1967), no. 25, pp. 44–47.

consensus on socialist principles is sufficiently ingrained to justify such a radical venture. Furthermore, this move to divest the League of direct-controlling power underscores the role of communists in Yugoslav society as a sort of overriding Brahmanic caste, in that they immunize themselves from the "dirty business" of politics and become the exclusive (and priestly) guardians of socialist morality. Here then it is presumed that social groups will be able to pursue their own interests and be "political" (without the direct assistance of the League) within the context of a broadly based Marxist commitment.

Recent developments in Yugoslav Marxist ideology point to a series of instructive trends. The Yugoslav domestic scene displays increasing evidence of variable ideological expression within the confines of a loose commitment to Marxist socialist principles. What distinguishes the Yugoslav system from other communist party states is precisely this ideological breadth or "looseness" within which the Yugoslav citizen might find political participation to be meaningful. The Yugoslavs still insist upon the continuous as well as the orthodox (but different) nature of their revolution, they persist in lauding their national liberation experience as an achievement of all Yugoslav peoples, and they underscore their commitment both to economic development and to basic Marxist end-values.[13] However, it is also stressed that a continuous revolution must be everywhere only experimental in nature and need not everywhere be the same; as a result, it is possible that a number of ideological variations (given a basic commitment to socialism) may serve as viable

[13]Puniša Perović, "Twenty-Five Years of the Yugoslav Revolution," *Socialist Thought and Practice* (1966), no. 22, pp. 23–28.

145

sources for recommending societal change. What remains uncertain here is the degree to which non-Marxist ideological postures will also be given legitimacy and will be allowed to intrude themselves into Yugoslav society.

The Yugoslav constitution promulgated in 1963 was designed to expand the involvement of the "working people" in the processes of direct democracy. The stated goal of this instrument was to turn the direction and management of social, economic, and political institutions over to the people themselves as "liberated personalities." Recently, a number of events have occurred that give concrete form to this general objective; the most important of these are the 1965 economic reforms, the April, 1967, elections, and the current reorganization of the League. Already having established law to the effect that elected officials may not succeed themselves (except for Tito), top Yugoslav leadership wanted to get more people more fully involved in the general system of sociopolitical institutions. In one sense, then, the Yugoslavs are working toward formal institutionalization of recognized conflict lines (through expanded participation) among various "social forces" within the context of a society based upon socialist principles.

Recent changes in the nature of Yugoslav economy had their theoretical backdrop formulated in 1964 during the Eighth Congress of the League of Communists.[14] The Yugoslav economic reforms that resulted

[14]Setting the mood for the new reforms, it was asserted at the Eighth Congress that "it is necessary to develop those forms of socialist productive and economic relations in general which, within the shortest time, will require ever fewer coercive measures for its own maintenance, and which will strengthen the

from this and that were legislated in July, 1965, focus upon two overriding concerns.[15] The first relates to bringing Yugoslav currency more in line with competitive Western units of monetary value. This required, first, a devaluation of the Yugoslav dinar (from 750 to 1,250 per dollar) and, second, the creation of a "new dinar" worth 100 times as much as the old. As a result, the new 12.5 dinar exchange rate for the American dollar was established as more "realistic" in that it met standards set by the international economy. The basic purpose was to put Yugoslav trade with Western countries upon a more viable and realistic foundation, with the hope of expanding such trade and making the new dinar acceptable to Western economies. The second concern relates to the reduced involvement of the Yugoslav federal government in matters dealing with economic investment and income distribution within the country.[16] This was reflected in a revised tax system that reduced the scope of direct government con-

---

possibility for developing more democratic and more humane relations among people." Edvard Kardelj, "Društveno-ekonomski zadaci privrednog razvoja u narednom periodu" ("Socio-Economic Tasks of Economic Development in the Forthcoming Period"), *Osmi kongres Saveza komunista Jugoslavije (Eighth Congress of the League of Communists of Yugoslavia)* (Beograd: Komunist, 1964), p. 70.

[15]For basic texts relating to the reform and relevant commentary, see: *Borba,* July 25, 1965.

[16]Official figures indicate that only 22 per cent of total Yugoslav capital investment is currently initiated by the state. The Yugoslav position is rather explicitly committed to reducing the area of state investment to certain essential aspects of industry and economy. The balance of the investment would be left with "work organizations," enterprises, commercial banks, and regional political entities. Petar Stambolić, "Toward a Modern Organization of the Economy," *Socialist Thought and Practice* (1966), no. 23, pp. 12–13.

trol and increased the ability of individual enterprises to finance their own operations.[17] In general, the economic reform has intensified two already existing trends: first, to stress indirect federal and republican controls through the tax structure and the banking system; and, second, to increase the privileges of local enterprises and communes to expend monies that are made in their own regions. The latter has had the problematic result during the short period since passage of the reforms of further increasing the differential rates of economic growth between the Yugoslav developed north and its underdeveloped south. This policy of encouraging regional economic autonomy has also intensified economically based conflicts among the various ethnocultural regions of the country. In general, the new Yugoslav reforms stress economic regional self-reliance (if an enterprise is inefficient, it should go bankrupt), which means that they are also designed "to allow fuller play to economic laws on the domestic market."[18] The result has been to underscore the market mechanism, enterprise and regional autonomy, and economic competition even more so than earlier, whereas on the other side it has tended to minimize the subsidizing of inefficient forms of enterprise and to discourage state involvement in the economy in general. Despite the short lapse of time since their in-

[17]Yugoslav social scientists have made extensive studies of the public response in Yugoslavia to the new economic reforms. On the whole, the evidence that they submit, based upon modern survey research techniques, indicates that the Yugoslav citizen strongly approves of these reforms. Firdus Džinić, ed., *Jugoslovensko javno mnenje o privrednoj reformi 1965 (Yugoslav Public Opinion on the Economic Reforms 1965* (Beograd: Institut društvenih nauka, 1965), esp. pp. 57–60.

[18]Stambolić, "Modern Organization of the Economy," p. 8.

ception, the Yugoslav economic reforms thus far show clear evidence of enjoying a measure of success, especially as reflected in growing personal income and social product in addition to a more favorable balance of payments.[19] From the standpoint of the goal of encouraging wider (and more democratic) participation in productive relations the consensus among Yugoslav leaders is that they have also achieved a measure of success.

In July, 1966, the Fourth Plenary Session of the Central Committee of the League of Communists took three steps of major import to Yugoslav political life. These included the forced resignation of Ranković as Vice-President of Yugoslavia under Tito, the commitment to reform and weaken the state security service, and the decision to reorganize the League of Communists.[20] A number of critical implications follow from these developments. First of all, the ouster of Ranković stems directly from the problem of attempting to implement and administer the new economic reforms.[21] The charge was made that Ranković and his cohorts had used the state security service in order to protect "conservatism" or, stated otherwise, to put roadblocks in the

[19]For an early, and rather cautious, Yugoslav assessment of the effects of these new economic measures, see: "Economic Reform and the Results of Economic Development in 1965," *Yugoslav Survey* (1966), no. 26, pp. 3781–92.

[20]Relevant documents and debate on these crictical issues are given in: "Fourth Plenum of the Central Committee of the League of Communists of Yugoslavia," *Socialist Thought and Practice* (1966), no. 23, pp. 103–41.

[21]For a useful Western interpretation of the demise of Ranković, see: R. V. Burks, *The Removal of Ranković: An Early Interpretation of the July Yugoslav Party Plenum* (Memorandum RM-5132-PR, August, 1966, The Rand Corporation, Santa Monica, California).

149

way of giving full effect to the new economic measures. Here then the demotion of Ranković could be tied directly to the problem of regional economic competition and its strongly ethnocultural aspect; in fact, during the Third Plenary Session of the Central Committee, Ranković apparently had been required by the League to admonish "certain Communists in Serbia" for resisting the implementation of the 1965 economic reforms.[22] The overriding issue of a struggle for power and succession was also raised by the Ranković ouster, with the added indictment made by Tito himself that recent events were much like "what used to happen under Stalin."[23] In addition to the charge that Ranković and others might have been involved in a power play, the criticism was generally made of the security police that it was placing itself above both the League and the society as a whole. As a result, the major effect of the Ranković affair was to make the state security service "responsible" by limiting its activities to protecting Yugoslav society against the "class enemy" and "external threats." Stated otherwise, the leadership of the League had been threatened and was given a scare, and now it wanted to assure that future activity of the state security service would be controlled by properly constituted authority. Finally, the Ranković dismissal (that is, forced resignation) had the added by-product of obscuring the succession problem in Yugoslavia, since most Western observers had felt for some time that Ranković was the obvious heir apparent to Tito.

A far-reaching set of *Draft Theses* concerning the

[22]Alexandar Ranković, "The Reform is Consolidating the Unity of the People," *Socialist Thought and Practice* (1966), no. 21, pp. 101–02.

[23]"Fourth Plenum of the Central Committee," p. 107.

reorganization of the League (although in fact anticipated to a large degree) seems to follow in the wake of the Ranković affair.[24] The basic motive underlying these League reforms relates to applying the principles of self-management and direct democracy that are believed to exist in Yugoslav society at large to the narrower confines of the League itself. A more specific theme focuses upon the abolition of "the 'personal' union between the leading forms of the League of Communists and the government," which means that leading political figures in Yugoslavia may not hold positions of power both in the government and in the League.[25] The result has been to put the League of Communists above both politics and government in the sense of existing as a nonparty or above-factions institution; in this regard, the League would function primarily as the caretaker of the basic socialist morality and Marxist principles that underlie Yugoslav society. However, the "divorcing of the party from power" requires from the other side that individual communists become more active politically since the direct party-control aspect in Yugoslav society would be expected to be minimized.[26] Here then the issue that might be

[24]For relevant materials and related discussions on most recent developments, see: *Komunist,* June 29, 1967; and Mijalko Todorović, "Reorganizacija Saveza komunista i objektivna potreba radničke klase" ("Reorganization of the League of Communists and Objective Needs of the Working Class"), *Komunist,* July 6, 1967.

[25]Crvenkovski, "Divorcing the Party from Power," p. 43; and *Komunist,* February 9, 1967.

[26]In this context, however, the question of the capability and dedication of League members has been raised in order (most probably) to encourage more active involvement in politics and organs of self-administration by members of the League. *Komunist,* July 27, 1967.

raised with respect to one-party versus multi-party systems is felt to be resolvable in favor of a *non-party system* where the "working people" and their organizations involve themselves directly in political life. In addition, the anticipated League reforms underscore the role that the Socialist Alliance will play in expanding participation and realizing direct democracy—that is, involving the Yugoslav citizen more fully in the activity of various sociopolitical institutions. As regards the internal democracy of the League itself, the *Draft Theses* stress the fact that open debate and criticism must be encouraged; more concretely, it is suggested that personal and collective resignation from the League might be honored without the normally expected punitive measures. What this seems to point toward is the development of a system of accountability in which members could legally resign as a form of protest against the policies that the League may be currently pursuing. As of the moment, it is difficult to say precisely what the concrete outcome of any such reforms might be, or which of the various debatable theses will be effectively implemented by future League congresses or Central Committee plenums. In any event, the basic thesis of "divorcing the party from power" and the internal democratization of the League are of and by themselves quite revolutionary even if they remain so merely in conception.

The recent April, 1967, elections are symptomatic of the far-reaching effects of increased liberalization of Yugoslav society as a whole.[27] Relevant aspects of these

[27]Analyses of the earlier 1965 elections have shown that trends that become quite clear in the more recent elections (for example, multi-candidate, competitive elections) were already beginning to appear. For example, see: R. V. Burks and S. A. Stanković, "Jugoslawien auf dem Weg zu halbfreien Wahlen?" *Osteuropa*, XVII (1967), 131–46.

elections include the encouraging of socioeconomic (and "work") organizations to put forth as many candidates as possible, the giving of concrete effect to the new constitutional provision calling for the nonsuccession (that is, rotation) of political offices, and the attempt to stimulate the participation of younger and more qualified candidates in general elections.[28] Preliminary analyses of election results have already indicated that these goals have been very largely attained. First of all, it appears that of the newly elected members of both federal and republican assemblies only a handful are carry-overs from previous legislative bodies. But what is even more important, those individuals who were selected for key governmental posts (for example, President of the Federal Assembly) reveal the emergence of a new, younger bevy of Yugoslav leaders. Both these developments give evidence that the principle of rotating political offices has been relatively effective. In fact, it appears that even well-known political figures such as Edvard Kardelj and Petar Stambolić do not hold key offices in either the executive or the legislative bodies at the federal level, although they still maintain influential positions in their respective republics as well as in top League organizations. Not surprisingly, the most noteworthy exception to the nonsuccession principle is Tito, who holds his job as president of Yugoslavia for the duration of his life. The nonsuccession rule does not of course mean that men such as Kardelj or Stambolić will lose their power and influence; it merely signifies that they will have to operate from a somewhat different or modified institutional basis than previously. Secondly, the recent Yugoslav elections have apparently expanded meaningful

[28]Edvard Kardelj, "Responsibility for the Elections," *Socialist Thought and Practice* (1967), no. 25, pp. 18, 26–27.

involvement in the political process by the Yugoslav citizenry in general as well as by the various socio-political organizations. Consequently, a considerably larger number of elections than was previously the case were multicandidate and were in fact competitively contested; even at the federal level we find that approximately 25 per cent of the available legislative seats had more than one candidate in the running, a proportion that becomes even greater at the lower commune level of government. A thought-provoking by-product of this more interested citizen participation in Yugoslav elections has been the loss of assembly seats by well-regarded League members to candidates not officially sanctioned by the League in highly competitive campaigns. The intensity and the nature of campaigning in the April, 1967, elections suggest in fact that the attractiveness of the candidate may gradually be taking precedence over the simple loyalty of the League member.[29] And, finally, the April electoral campaign has resulted in salient changes in the basic sociological make-up of the Yugoslav leadership structure. Generally, the elections have favored the younger men with better education over the older ones with more experience, the younger partisan fighters of the resistance over the older, pre-World War II communists, and the well-trained manager or professional over the older party "hack" or *aparatčik*. In short, the April, 1967, elections have fully established the vanguard of a more

[29]The presumption of the League of Communists has been that the intelligent, well-informed vote would in any event tend to be cast for the League member. *Komunist,* January 12, 1967. However, this may well be a miscalculation as regards the level of consensus on socialist principles, a consensus that may not as yet be sufficiently developed in Yugoslavia to assure a "right choice" in the voting booth.

sophisticated, professional, urbane, educated, and youthful leadership element. Throughout all this, however, the League itself has still maintained the necessary strategic ethnocultural balance in its leadership composition in order to assure the representation of major national groups within the country. Given the long history of strife among Yugoslav national groups, such a policy affords an eminently reasonable tactic for holding ethnocultural conflict in check.

Two overriding aspects of the Yugoslav pattern of foreign relations have centered on the problems of the nonaligned world and the continued expansion of trade relations with the West. In the tradition of the earlier Belgrade and Cairo conferences of nonaligned states, a summit meeting of the "big three" of the non-aligned bloc (that is, Tito, Nasser, and Gandhi) was held in October, 1966, at New Delhi. In addition to reaffirming the basic commitment to nonalignment by the less developed nations, the meeting expressed deep concern for the Vietnam war and what was felt to be the generally worsening situation of the developing world.[30] Focal here was what was viewed as a renewed surge of foreign pressures and the usual subtle forms of "imperialist" exploitation on the part of the larger and, especially, the Western powers. In this context, the Yugoslav regime continued to pursue its policy of strengthening its own position of influence in world politics independent of either power bloc, striving to do this by the cultivation of friends and supporters among the disenchanted of the underdeveloped sphere. On this point, studies have in fact demonstrated that voting patterns of the Yugoslav delegation to the

[30]Milan Draškić, "Tripartite Meeting and the Asian Situation," *Socialist Thought and Practice* (1966), no. 24, pp. 156–59.

United Nations more closely follow the Afro-Asian constellation of nations than they do those of either the Communist or the Western Bloc.[31] These traditionally established attitudes of the Yugoslav regime have also had their impact upon the Arab-Israeli (June, 1967) conflict in the Middle East. On the whole, the Yugoslavs were unambiguous in their insistence upon the flagrantly aggressive designs of Israel against the Arab world.[32] In addition, consistent with the theme of the nonaligned world in general, the Yugoslav regime has stressed the "imperialistic" aspects of the Middle East conflict, with the not unexpected indictment of both Great Britain and the United States. What followed in concrete behavioral terms was a strong verbal denunciation by Tito of Israeli aggression in addition to the formal severance of diplomatic relations with Israel. Rather curiously, the Israeli problem has also become a conflict-provoking domestic Yugoslav issue; mutterings are heard suggesting that Tito had acted too rashly and without consulting the proper ministries of government. The basic concern expressed by domestic critics is that Yugoslavia should have properly maintained a neutralist and moderate (that is, "nonaligned") position in the Middle East crisis. Instructive here is that the judgment of Tito himself has been at least indirectly challenged regarding his somewhat rash actions in the Arab-Israeli conflict by an influential sector of Yugoslav leadership. Furthermore, the visit by the Yugoslav president in June, 1967, to Moscow has also

[31]On Yugoslav voting patterns in the United Nations, see: Bruce M. Russett, "Discovering Voting Groups in the United Nations," *The American Political Science Review,* LX (June, 1966), pp. 327–39.

[32]*Komunist,* June 29, 1967.

been questioned by a number of Yugoslav leaders, since it was felt that such an unprecedented move could be interpreted in the West as an indicator that Yugoslavia is moving back into the communist orbit. Although the eventual outcome at this point remains quite uncertain, it is clear that a salient division (which is becoming increasingly manifest) exists within Yugoslav leadership circles regarding current world problems. Tito it would appear has been caught in the cross fire between his commitment, on the one hand, to Nasser and the nonaligned, anti-imperialist world in general and, on the other, to certain influential forces within Yugoslavia that want to see even closer ties (especially economic ones) with the Western world. In any event, it seems likely that politically the Yugoslavs will continue to tread the fine line between East and West and will try to hold on to their prestigious role as leaders of the nonaligned world.

In contrast to what seems to be suggested by Tito's recent visit to Moscow, the Yugoslav trade pattern continues to show stronger inclinations toward the West. In fact, a major goal of the 1965 economic reforms was precisely to make the Yugoslav dinar a convertible and an acceptable currency in Western countries. Evidence also suggests that, as the Yugoslav trade position vis-à-vis the West improves, its relations (from an economic standpoint) become increasingly difficult and strained with other communist party states. Apparently, the decision to trade with the countries of East Europe continues to be viewed as a "political" one, while individual Yugoslav enterprises themselves are lobbying vigorously for extending economic contacts with the West. A number of specific events of recent vintage suggest this continued trend toward economic contact

157

with the West. First, the Yugoslav regime has apparently conceded to inviting foreign investment funds into Yugoslavia with the normal expectation that profits can be accumulated. Consistent with this, official Yugoslav policy now encourages the creation of as many joint economic ventures between foreign (that is, Western) business concerns and individual enterprises as prove economically feasible.[33] Second, regarding the import-export balance, the Yugoslavs continue to find themselves in an unfavorable situation vis-à-vis Western economies, whereas they still maintain a favorable balance of trade with both the less developed and the communist world.[34] Third, an important recent change has been the gradually increasing volume of private imports by Yugoslav citizens (Trieste has been referred to as "the supermarket of Slovenia") as against the import of goods by socially owned or state enterprises. Such a trend would of course suggest a further intensification of direct contact between the individual Yugoslav consumer and the foreign entrepreneur and wholesaler. Fourth, the foreign tourist trade continues to become increasingly important for the Yugoslav economy with each passing year as larger numbers of Westerners flow into the country for short visits.[35] A significant by-product of this development has been a

[33] Jose Korošec, "Greater Incentive to Dealing with Foreign Firms," *Yugoslav Export,* September 1, 1966.

[34] Recent figures indicate a strong increase in Yugoslav exports which has reduced its normally unfavorable import-export differential. Mihovil Kapetanić, "Increased Exports and Economic Growth," *Yugoslav Export,* August 1, 1967.

[35] Tourism has developed so rapidly and to such an extent that Yugoslavs publicly complain that there is little room left for the "Yugoslav tourist" in the more popular areas such as the Adriatic Coast after the uncontrolled wave of foreign tourists arrives. *Komunist,* August 3, 1967.

relaxation by the Yugoslav regime of restrictions upon (and even the encouragement of) various forms of private catering services and privately owned tourist enterprises in the country. And, finally, regarding the flow of Yugoslavs into Western countries, Yugoslavia continues to be a major exporter of unskilled (and to some degree even skilled) human manpower resources. The latest reports in fact indicate that over 250,000 Yugoslavs hold temporary jobs in various West European countries. Since these working Yugoslavs usually return to their home country after rather brief sojourns abroad, they provide an important channel both for Western hard currency and Western cultural influence in general. Although without direct relevance to economic trends in the country, it should also be noted that the Yugoslav regime has normalized its relations with the Vatican to allow for the exchange of diplomatic representatives.[36] Given the sizable Catholic population in Yugoslavia, this diplomatic move by the communist regime also has its important domestic implications. All these factors point to intensified Yugoslav exposure to the noncommunist Western world, a trend that seems to be especially apparent in matters relating to economy and trade. In view of this general trend, the seemingly expanded Yugoslav "political" contact in recent months with communist party states (especially the Moscow visit by Tito) might be noted as an exercise in counterpoint.

The assessment of recent developments suggests that the Yugoslav system could well move in a number of directions. It has become rather clear that a significant measure of ideological diversity and tolerance does in fact now exist and is even encouraged within the coun-

[36]*Yugoslav News Bulletin,* June 27, 1966.

try.[37] Whether this will evolve to a point that will permit openly non-Marxist (or even anti-Marxist) movements, or if it will allow the formation of an organized political opposition, remains a problematic future development. However, the release of Milovan Djilas from confinement in addition to the rather gentle treatment of both Ranković and Mihajlov may well be indicative of things to come. If one takes more or less at face value what both the new economic reforms and the planned League reorganization specify, then it seems that Yugoslavia could well emerge as perhaps the first multi-party (but still a Marxian) socialist country. What is most intriguing here is the apparent internal contradiction between, on the one hand, the irresistible trends in Yugoslav economy and, on the other, the sluggish adaptation of its policy. In fact, this tension between economy and polity has become so salient recently that Yugoslavs themselves observe that elements constituting the "opposition" within the Federal Assembly are those who present economic (and not ideological-political) forms of argument to support their cases. The economically motivated continue to pull strongly toward the West, whereas the politically motivated seem to be attracted more so by the East. Furthermore, this overriding cleavage was best dramatized in the recent visit by Tito to Moscow and the concern it generated within Yugoslavia among the more economically minded sectors of Yugoslav leadership. It goes without saying that as the Yugoslav system continues to open up to the West for economic pur-

[37]Mika Tripalo, "Savremena integraciona kretanja zahtevaju idejnu diferencijaciju" ("The Contemporary Process of Integration Requires Ideological Differentiation"), *Komunist,* June 29, 1967.

poses, and as the attributes of a modernized society take deeper hold, it will most likely also have to make the appropriate adjustments in its ideological-political forms as well. The only question that remains is whether the more militant elements among Yugoslav leadership circles will tolerate what appears to be a logical and natural path of development for the country.

CONCLUSION

As stated at the outset of this study, the focus has been upon the dynamics of development in communist-based societies. Those conditions that evoke both ideological and institutional changes were therefore of crucial importance to the investigation. In addition, and perhaps even more crucial, the general efforts have been centered upon the specific nature of such changes. Stemming from the need to confront unique problems in social experimentation, communist-based systems tend to differentiate themselves from one another with respect to institutional and ideological forms that are adopted. The pattern in Yugoslavia was to move from a deeply felt reliance upon a purist Soviet model of a "socialist society" to a more qualified model, in fact one rather severely contaminated by apparent "capitalistic" and pluralist elements. The result was to create within the Yugoslav system institutional and ideological forms apparently quite different from those found in other socialist or communist states. And, even further, it resulted in the development of an internal political environment that invites a certain degree of ideological diversity and even debate. In Yugoslavia, the loosening of domestic constraints (both ideologically and politically) was paralleled externally by expansion and diversification of trade patterns and other foreign ties. As a result, the Yugoslavs have not for some time viewed themselves as members of any so-called Soviet or, for that matter, any other type of bloc, except to align themselves firmly with the growing but loose array of "third world" nation states. In fact, they are deeply insulted and react strongly to the suggestion that they owe their behavior to bloc pressures emanating from any sector of the world. The proposition that internal liberalization corresponds with external diversification and balanced relations appears to hold true in the Yugoslav case.

Historically, scholarly research in the communist field has perhaps given too much weight to a single variable—namely, the existence of a communist party regime. The dangers stemming from such a limited approach include overlooking and selling short other equally salient factors operative in the system and overall environment which modify its functioning and structure. Scientific procedure would require that, if predictability is to be maximized, a certain range of relevant variables must be included in the analytic model. The difficulty with the traditional "communist monolith" model is that it is far too simple and, further, that it seeks all its answers through essentially one aspect of a far more intricate and complex phenomenon. In short, it quite simply fails to account for or to explain any number of crucial variables, many of which are related to "Marxism" in only the most obscure way; all such variables without doubt would bear significantly on the course of development of the system in question. There is in fact good reason to believe that there are many so-called noncommunist variables that will have their telling effects upon Yugoslav society or, for that matter, upon any socialist or communist party state. The thrust of this study has been precisely to demonstrate the need for a more complex model for more effective analysis of communist-based systems. The intricacies of Yugoslav institutional and experiential patterns defy simple analysis and the time-worn concepts so frequently employed in the field of communist studies. The immense professional task that now remains (and it is hoped at least partially achieved here) envisions a fuller and more systematic development of an analytic model appropriate for investigating Marxist-based societies taken in the broadest sense.

APPENDIX: SELECTED DATA TABLES

TABLE 1

Yugoslav Population According to Nationality

National Group	1931[1]		1948[2]		1953[3]		1961[4]	
	000's	%	000's	%	000's	%	000's	%
Serbs	10,731	77.0	6,547	41.5	7,066	41.7	7,806	42.1
Croats	_a_	_a_	3,784	24.0	3,976	23.5	4,294	23.7
Slovenes	1,135	8.2	1,415	9.0	1,487	8.8	1,589	8.6
Macedonians	_a_	_a_	810	5.1	893	5.3	1,045	5.6
Moslem Slavs (_Muslimani_)	_a_	_a_	—	—	—	—	973	5.2
Yugoslavs undeclared	_a_	_a_	809[b]	5.1	999[b]	5.9	317	1.7
Albanians	505	3.6	750	4.8	754	4.4	914	4.9
Hungarians (Magyars)	468	3.4	496	3.2	502	3.0	504	2.7
Montenegrins	_a_	_a_	426	2.7	466	2.8	514	2.8
Vlachs	_c_	_c_	103	0.7	37	0.2	—	—
Turks	133	0.9	98	0.6	260	1.5	182	0.9
Slovaks	76	0.5	84	0.5	85	0.5	86	0.4

Italians	9	0.1	80	0.5	36	0.2	26	0.1
Gypsies	70	0.5	73	0.5	85	0.5	—	—
Rumanians	138	1.0	64	0.4	60	0.3	61	0.3
Bulgars	a	a	61	0.4	62	0.4	63	0.3
Germans	500	3.6	55	0.4	61	0.4	—	—
Czechs	53	0.4	39	0.2	35	0.2	30	0.1
Ruthenians	—	—	—	—	37	0.2	—	—
Russians	36	0.3	20	0.2	12	0.1	—	—
Others and undetermined	—	—	20	0.2	14	0.1	143	0.7
Total	13,934	100.0	15,772	100.0	16,937	100.0	18,549	100.0

[a] Listed as Serbo-Croats or "Serbs" in this Table.

[b] Yugoslav Moslems living in Bosnia-Hercegovina were allowed to refuse to identify themselves as either Serb or Croat and usually chose the "Yugoslav undeclared" category.

[c] The Vlachs were probably combined with Rumanians for this census.

[1] George W. Hoffman and Fred W. Neal, *Yugoslavia and the New Communism* (New York: Twentieth Century Fund, 1962), p. 29.

[2] Savezni zavod za statistiku i evidenciju (Federal Bureau of Statistics and Evidence), *Konačni rezultati popisa stanovništva od 15 Marta 1948 godine (Final Results of the Population Census of 15 March 1948)* (Beograd, 1954), IX, xiv-xv, xl-xlii.

[3] Savezni zavod za statistiku (Federal Bureau of Statistics), *Popis stanovništva 1953. Narodnost i maternji jezik (Population Census 1953. Nationality and Mother-Tongue)* (Beograd, 1959), VIII, 92-98.

[4] Savezni zavod za statistiku (Federal Bureau of Statistics), *Statistički bilten (Statistical Bulletin)*, no. 250 (Beograd, 1962), p. 13.

Table 2

Distribution of 1953 Population by Nationality According to Republics[1]

National Group[2]	Yugoslavia	Serbia				Croatia	Slovenia	Bosnia-Hercegovina	Macedonia	Montenegro
		All	Proper	Vojvodina	Kosmet					
Serbs	41.7	73.8	91.7	51.1	23.5	15.0	0.8	44.4	2.7	3.3
Croats	23.5	2.5	0.9	7.5	0.8	79.6	1.2	23.0	0.2	2.3
Slovenes	8.8	0.5	0.3	0.4	0.1	1.1	96.5	0.2	0.1	0.2
Macedonians	5.3	0.4	0.3	0.7	0.1	0.1	0.0	0.1	66.0	0.1
Montenegrins	2.7	1.2	0.6	1.8	3.9	0.1	0.1	0.3	0.2	86.6
Moslem Slavs (*Muslimani*)	5.9	1.2	1.5	0.6	0.8	0.4	0.1	31.3	0.1	1.5
Albanians	4.5	8.1	0.9	0.1	64.9	0.0	0.0	0.1	12.5	5.6
Hungarians (Magyars)	3.0	6.3	0.1	25.4	0.0	1.2	0.8	0.0	0.0	0.0
Turks	1.5	0.8	0.4	0.0	4.3	0.0	0.0	0.0	15.6	0.1
Others	3.1	5.2	3.4	12.4	1.6	2.5	0.5	0.6	2.6	0.3

[1]Percentages for 1953 Census cited in: Savezni zavod za statistiku (Federal Bureau of Statistics), *Demografska statistika, 1959 (Demographic Statistics, 1959)* (Beograd, 1962), p. 26.

[2]The republics, ranked in order of homogeneity, are: Slovenia, 96.5 per cent (Slovenes); Montenegro, 86.6 per cent (Montenegrins); Croatia, 79.6 per cent (Croats); Serbia, 73.8 per cent (Serbs); Macedonia, 66.0 per cent (Macedonians); and Bosnia-Hercegovina, 44.4 per cent (Serbs).

TABLE 3

Population according to Religious Confession

Confession	1931[1] (000's)	(%)	1948[2] (000's)	(%)	1953[3] (000's)	(%)
Orthodox	6,784	48.70	7,833	49.53	6,985	41.20
Catholic	5,217	37.45	5,800	36.77	5,371	31.70
Protestant	241	1.74	157	1.14	157	0.93
Moslem	1,561	11.20	1,975	12.52	2,090	12.31
Other Christian	58	0.41	—	—	61	0.40
Jewish	68	0.49	6	0.04	2	0.01
Nonbelievers	1	0.01	—	—	2,128	12.50
Indifferent believers	—	—	—	—	10	0.05
Unknown	—	—	—	—	131	0.90
Total	13,934	100.00	15,772	100.00	16,936	100.00

[1]Ljubiša Stojkovič and Miloš Martić, *National Minorities in Yugoslavia* (Belgrade, 1952), pp. 30–31.

[2]*Ibid.*, p. 90. The 1948 Census did not obtain data on religious confession. These figures are interpolations derived from percentages given in Stojković and Martić.

[3]Savezni zavod za statistiku (Federal Bureau of Statistics), *Popis stanovništva (Population Census)* (Beograd, 1959), I, 278–79.

TABLE 4

Population Growth-Indicators

Year	Birth Rate	Death Rate	Natural Increase	Infant Mortality
	(per 1,000)	(per 1,000)	(per 1,000)	(per 1,000)
1931[1]	33.6	19.8	13.8	164.5
1948[1]	28.1	13.5	14.6	102.1[2]
1953[1]	28.4	12.4	16.0	116.1
1957[1]	23.9	10.7	13.2	101.5
1961[1]	22.6	9.0	13.6	82.2
1963[3]	21.4	8.9	12.5	77.5
1964[4]	20.8	9.4	11.4	77.5

[1]Savezni zavod za statistiku (Federal Bureau of Statistics), *Statistički godišnjak FNRJ, 1962 (Statistical Yearbook FPRY, 1962)* (Beograd, 1962), p. 54.

[2]No figures were available for 1948 on infant mortality; this figure is based upon 1949 data.

[3]Federal Institute of Statistics, *Yugoslavia 1958–1964, Statistical Data* (Beograd, n.d.), pp. 20–21.

[4]Savezni zavod za statistiku (Federal Bureau of Statistics), *Statistički kalendar Jugoslavije, 1965 (Statistical Pocketbook of Yugoslavia, 1965)* (Beograd, 1965), pp. 30–31.

TABLE 5 (Part 1)

Distribution of Population According to Activity[1]
1931

Activity	Active	Dependent	Total	%
Industry, handicrafts, and mining	704,548	816,050	1,520,598	11.0
Agriculture	5,095,686	5,571,677	10,667,363	76.5
Trade, transportation, and banking	254,685	403,617	658,302	4.6
Public service, free professions, and military	285,053	262,066	547,119	3.9
Other occupations	277,645	263,011	530,656	4.0
Total	6,617,617	7,316,421	13,939,038	100.0

[1]Kraljevina Jugoslavija (Kingdom of Yugoslavia), *Statistički godišnjak, 1936 (Statistical Yearbook, 1936)* (Beograd: Janićijević, 1937), pp. 32–35. For a discussion of population dependent on agriculture for this period and of active-dependent population generally, see: Jozo Tomasevich, *Peasants, Politics, and Economic Change in Yugoslavia* (Stanford, Calif.: Stanford University Press, 1955), pp. 303–7.

TABLE 5 (Part 2)

Distribution of Population According to Activity[1]

Activity	1953				1961			
	Active	Dependent	Total	%	Active	Dependent	Total	%
Mining	112,277	210,066	322,343	1.9	144,673	307,276	451,949	2.4
Industry	512,702	627,904	1,140,606	6.7	993,175	1,198,081	2,191,256	11.8
Agriculture	5,182,521	4,923,066	10,105,587	59.6	4,674,856	4,494,908	9,169,764	49.4
Forestry	57,942	112,727	170,669	1.0	73,268	155,156	228,424	1.2
Construction	205,555	325,174	530,726	3.1	317,525	528,045	845,570	4.5
Transportation	167,955	327,439	495,394	2.9	249,698	454,063	703,761	3.7
Trade	162,447	244,525	407,972	2.4	226,013	270,499	496,512	2.6
Handicraft	365,770	470,531	836,301	4.9	378,908	472,011	850,919	4.5
State administration and justice	219,748	350,877	570,625	3.3	182,130	287,008	469,138	2.5
Education, culture, and science	122,846	115,942	238,788	1.4	212,459	180,497	392,956	2.1
Health and social welfare	73,932	62,733	136,665	0.8	142,826	111,391	254,117	1.3
Persons with private income	541,781	363,901	905,682	5.3	684,428	464,721	1,149,149	6.1
All others	665,165	411,062	1,076,227	6.3	744,869	600,207	1,345,076	7.2
Total	8,390,638	8,545,935	16,936,573	100.0	9,024,828	9,524,463	18,549,291	100.0

TABLE 6

Index of Industrial Production and Selected Industries[1]

Year	Index of Industrial Production	Electrical Energy (million kw-h.)	Coal (thousand M.T.)	Crude Iron (thousand M.T.)	Value of Construction (million dinars)
1939	100.0	1,173	7,032[2]	101	—
1948	150.3	2,061	10,644	171	—
1953	182.6	2,982	11,247	270	179,091
1957	311.0	6,252	18,007	214	235,318
1961	483.4	9,924	24,037	997	600,761
1963	596.0	13,535	27,422	996	735,233

[1] Figures for 1939–61 are from: Savezni zavod za statistiku (Federal Bureau of Statistics), *Statistički godišnjak FNRJ, 1962* (*Statistical Yearbook FPRY, 1962*) (Beograd, 1962), pp. 142–44; those for 1963 and for "Value of Construction" are from: *Statistical Yearbook, 1964*, pp. 177–78, 198.

[2] This figure includes the production of the Raše mine, which belonged to Italy during this early period.

TABLE 7
Agricultural Production and Selected Commodities[1]

Year	Index of Agricultural Production[2]	Wheat ('000 T.)	Wheat (per hectare)	Tobacco ('000 T.)	Tobacco (per hectare)	Potatoes ('000 T.)	Potatoes (per hectare)	Mutton ('000 T.)
1939	104	2,910,000	13.1	16,500	10.3	1,540,000	54	65
1948	107	2,530,000[3]	13.4	29,300[4]	8.6	1,480,000[5]	75	23[6]
1953	110	2,510,000	13.3	30,900	8.6	2,100,000	84	52
1957	145	3,100,000	15.8	63,300	11.2	3,310,000	115	56
1961	147	3,170,000	16.1	15,000	5.7	2,690,000	91	54
1963	165[7]	4,140,000	19.3	54,000	10.2	3,020,000	93	48

[1]Figures for 1939–61 are from: Savezni zavod za statistiku (Federal Bureau of Statistics), *Statistički godišnjak FNRJ, 1962* (*Statistical Yearbook FPRJ, 1962*) (Beograd, 1962), pp. 107–22; those for 1963 are from *Statistical Yearbook, 1964*, pp. 143–52.

[2]The base-index of 100 derives from an average for the years 1947–56. The 1939 index constitutes an average for the years 1930–39.

[3]*Statistical Yearbook, 1955*, p. 112.

[4]*Statistical Yearbook, 1958*, p. 115.

[5]*Statistical Yearbook, 1955*, p. 116.

[6]*Statistical Yearbook, 1958*, p. 125.

[7]This represents an approximation based upon an index average for 1954–63 = 100.

TABLE 8 (Part 1)
Yugoslav Foreign Trade Pattern for Selected Countries

Countries	1938[1] Imp.	1938[1] Ex.	1947[2] Imp.	1947[2] Ex.	1953[3] Imp.	1953[3] Ex.	1957[4] Imp.	1957[4] Ex.	1961[4] Imp.	1961[4] Ex.	1963[5] Imp.	1963[5] Ex.
	(%)	(%)	(%)	(%)	(%)	(%)	(%)	(%)	(%)	(%)	(%)	(%)
Austria	6.9	6.0	3.1	5.0	6.4	6.4	3.7	4.8	3.5	4.5	3.0	3.5
Germany (West)	32.5	35.9	—	—	17.4	16.6	11.4	13.2	15.6	10.1	7.8	9.6
Italy	8.9	6.4	8.6	10.2	7.1	15.6	11.9	13.5	14.5	12.3	10.6	20.0
Britain	8.6	9.6	5.4	2.7	6.2	13.5	6.3	6.4	5.0	8.4	4.7	5.4
France	2.8	1.4	2.5	1.3	7.5	3.7	1.5	2.3	2.5	1.7	4.5	2.1
U.S.A.	6.0	5.0	4.0	0.1	34.4	13.9	26.2	8.6	19.5	6.4	17.6	5.8
U.S.S.R.	0.1	—	22.2	16.8	0.3[a]	0.8[a]	10.4	13.2	3.8	8.9	6.8	10.8
Czechoslovakia	10.6	7.8	17.6	18.8	0.3[a]	1.5[a]	2.8	2.1	2.1	2.9	4.0	2.9
Africa	—	—	0.2	1.7	1.1	3.1	2.2	5.2	2.3	4.6	4.8	8.3
Asia	—	—	—	—	2.9	2.5	5.9	7.3	4.9	9.9	7.9	8.3
Other	23.0	29.4	36.4	43.4	16.3	22.1	17.4	23.4	25.8	30.5	27.8	22.7

[a] Trade was not resumed with Communist Bloc countries until 1954; therefore 1954 figures are given here instead of those for 1953.

[1] Opšta državna statistika (General State Statistics), *Statistički godišnjak, 1938–39 Kraljevine Jugoslavije (Statistical Yearbook, 1938–39 Kingdom of Yugoslavia)* (Beograd, 1999), pp. 252–53.

[2] Savezni zavod za statistiku i evidenciju (Federal Bureau of Statistics and Evidence), *Statistika spoljne trgovine FNR Jugoslavije za 1946, 1947, 1948 i 1949 Godinu (Statistics on Foreign Trade of FPR Yugoslavia for 1946, 1947, 1948, and 1949)* (Beograd, 1953), pp. xiv–xv.

[3] Savezni zavod za statistiku (Federal Bureau of Statistics), *Statistički godišnjak FNRJ, 1955 (Statistical Yearbook FPRY, 1955)* (Beograd, 1955), p. 212.

[4] *Statistical Yearbook, 1962*, p. 188.

[5] Federal Institute of Statistics, *Yugoslavia 1958–1964, Statistical Data* (Beograd, n.d.), pp. 59–60.

TABLE 8 (Part 2)
Export-Import Balance

Years	Export Total	Import Total	Balance of Trade
	(*millions of dinars*)	(*millions of dinars*)	
1938	5,047	4,975	101
1948	55,794	118,591	47
1957	118,533	198,394	59
1961	170,670	273,087	62
1963	237,103	316,986	78
1964	267,733	396,953	68

TABLE 9
Tourist Trade of Yugoslavia from Selected Countries[1]

Countries	1938	1948	1953	1957	1961	1963
Austria	11,298	—	44,044	71,137	286,592	352,976
Germany (West)	135,972	3,318	56,898	120,511	236,620	439,850
Italy	13,477	—	17,619	40,322	100,350	186,524
Britain	13,106	1,140	31,003	36,551	70,911	124,136
France	8,831	635	19,308	57,186	88,786	138,748
U.S.A.	5,169	868	17,892	22,183	38,495	59,643
U.S.S.R.	—	—	—	8,368	7,663	14,720
Czechoslovakia	—	22,258	—	11,522	3,629	12,794
Poland	—	—	—	9,688	17,159	38,627
All countries	287,391	61,500	245,211	498,736	1,079,516	1,754,663

[1]Figures for 1938 are from: Savezni zavod za statistiku (Federal Bureau of Statistics), *Statistički godišnjak FNRJ, 1955* (*Statistical Yearbook FPRY, 1955*) (Beograd, 1955), pp. 240–41; those for 1948 are from *Statistical Yearbook, 1959*, p. 206; those for 1953–63 are from *Statistical Yearbook, 1964*, pp. 260–61.

SELECTED BIBLIOGRAPHY

Adamic, Louis. *My Native Land.* New York: Harper and Brothers, 1943.

Avakumovic, Ivan. *History of the Communist Party of Yugoslavia.* Aberdeen: The Aberdeen University Press, 1964.

Bass, Robert, and Marbury, Elizabeth, eds. *The Soviet-Yugoslav Controversy, 1948–1958: A Documentary Record.* New York: Prospect Books, 1959.

Brzezinski, Zbigniew K. *The Soviet Bloc—Unity and Conflict.* New York: Frederick A. Praeger, 1961.

Byrnes, R. F., ed. *Yugoslavia.* New York: Frederick A. Praeger, 1957.

Dedijer, Vladimir. *Tito.* New York: Simon and Schuster, 1953.

Dvornik, Francis. *The Slavs—Their Early History and Civilization.* Boston: American Academy of Arts and Sciences, 1956.

Heppell, Muriel, and Singleton, Frank B. *Yugoslavia.* New York: Frederick A. Praeger, 1961.

Hoffman, George W., and Neal, Fred W. *Yugoslavia and the New Communism.* New York: Twentieth Century Fund, 1962.

Hoptner, J. B. *Yugoslavia in Crisis, 1934–1941.* New York: Columbia University Press, 1962.

Kardelj, Edvard. *Socialism and War.* New York: McGraw-Hill Book Company, Inc., 1960.

Kerner, Robert J., ed. *Yugoslavia.* Berkeley, Calif.: University of California Press, 1949.

Marriot, J. A. R. *The Eastern Question.* Oxford: The Clarendon Press, 1917.

Neal, Fred W. *Titoism in Action.* Berkeley, Calif.: University of California Press, 1957.

Seton-Watson, Hugh. *The East European Revolution.* New York: Frederick A. Praeger, 1951.

Tomasevich, Jozo. *Peasants, Politics, and Economic Change in Yugoslavia.* Stanford, Calif.: Stanford University Press, 1954.

Trouton, Ruth. *Peasant Renaissance in Yugoslavia, 1900–1950.* London: Routledge and Kegan Paul, Ltd., 1952.

Ulam, Adam. *Titoism and the Cominform.* Cambridge, Mass.: Harvard University Press, 1952.

West, Rebecca. *Black Lamb and Grey Falcon.* New York: The Viking Press, 1941.

Wolff, Robert Lee. *The Balkans in Our Time.* Cambridge, Mass.: Harvard University Press, 1956.

Yugoslavia's Way—The Program of the League of the Communists of Yugoslavia. New York: All Nations Press, 1958.